THE CHATGPT GOLDRUSH: PROFITING FROM THE AI REVOLUTION

PROMPT ENGINEERING MASTERY WITH CHATGPT-4

TABLE OF CONTENTS

I. INTRODUCTION TO CHATGPT

WHAT IS CHATGPT?

ChatGPT is a large language model created by OpenAI based on the GPT-4 architecture. It is designed to understand and respond to natural language text input, allowing conversations to occur with a machine. ChatGPT has been trained on a vast amount of data, allowing it to generate coherent and contextually appropriate responses to a wide range of prompts. With its advanced natural language processing capabilities, ChatGPT has the ability to carry out tasks such as language translation, text summarization, and question answering.

APPLICATIONS OF CHATGPT

ChatGPT, as a large language model, has numerous applications in various fields, including but not limited to education, healthcare, customer service, and entertainment. In this part, we will discuss some of the most notable applications of ChatGPT and how they can be used to enhance various industries.

1. **Chatbots and Virtual Assistants -** One of the most common applications of ChatGPT is developing chatbots and virtual assistants. With its advanced natural language processing capabilities, ChatGPT can be used to create chatbots that can understand and respond to human input. These chatbots can be used in various industries, from customer service to healthcare, to help users find information, answer questions, and solve problems.

2. **Language Translation -** ChatGPT can also be used to develop language translation tools. With its ability to understand and generate text in

1

multiple languages, ChatGPT can be used to create translation tools that can accurately translate text from one language to another. This application can be especially useful in international business and diplomacy industries.

3. **Text Summarization** – It can also be used to develop text summarization tools to help users understand the main points of a long text quickly and without difficulty. This application can be useful in journalism, where reporters need to summarize a news story for their audience quickly.

4. **Question Answering** - ChatGPT can be used to create question-answering tools that can help users find information quickly and easily. These tools can be used in various industries, from education to customer service, to help users find the answers to their questions without having to search through long documents or websites.

5. **Personalized Content Generation** - ChatGPT can also generate personalized content for users based on their interests and preferences. This application can be used in industries such as marketing and entertainment to create targeted advertising and content that is more likely to engage and retain users.

6. **Education** - ChatGPT can be used in education to create personalized learning experiences for students. By analyzing student data and generating personalized content, ChatGPT can help students learn at their own pace and in a way best suited to their learning style.

7. **Healthcare** - Also, in healthcare, ChatGPT can be used to help doctors and nurses quickly and accurately diagnose patients. ChatGPT can help healthcare professionals make more informed decisions and provide better patient care by analyzing patient data and generating possible diagnoses.

8. **Entertainment** - ChatGPT can also create interactive entertainment experiences, such as chat-based games and virtual reality experiences. This application can be used in the gaming and social media industries to create engaging and immersive user experiences.

9. **Customer Support** - ChatGPT can be used in customer service in a variety of ways, including:

Automated customer support: ChatGPT can be trained to answer frequently asked questions and provide solutions to common problems. This can be done through a chatbot interface, where customers can interact with ChatGPT in real-time to get the help they need.

Personalized customer interactions: ChatGPT can also be used to personalize customer interactions. By analyzing customer data and past interactions, ChatGPT can provide personalized recommendations, promotions, and offers tailored to each customer.

Multilingual customer support: ChatGPT can provide multilingual customer support. By using ChatGPT, businesses can offer customer support in languages other than the primary language of their customer base.

24/7 customer support: ChatGPT can also provide 24/7 customer support. Unlike human customer support representatives, ChatGPT can work around the clock to assist customers with their queries and issues.

Overall, ChatGPT can be a valuable tool for businesses looking to enhance their customer service capabilities and improve customer satisfaction.

Seeing how ChatGPT has multiple different uses, it is important to learn how to utilize this platform to achieve your business goals.

II: WHAT CAN I USE CHATGPT FOR?

CONTENT CREATION

Content creation refers to producing and sharing information, ideas, and other forms of media for a specific audience. It can include creating written content such as blog posts, articles, and social media posts, as well as visual content such as images, infographics, and videos.

The goal of content creation is typically to inform, entertain, or educate an audience to build a relationship and engage with them. Content creation can be done for many purposes, such as promoting a product or service, building brand awareness, establishing thought leadership, or simply sharing information and insights.

Content creators work in various industries, including marketing, journalism, education, and entertainment. They also use a range of tools and platforms to create and distribute their content, such as social media, blogs, podcasts, and video-sharing sites.

ELEMENTS OF CONTENT CREATION

Content creation is an essential aspect of digital marketing. It involves creating and sharing online content such as blog posts, videos, social media posts, images, infographics, and more. It can help businesses build their brand, drive traffic to their website, and engage with their audience. In this part, we will explain the elements of content creation and how to utilize ChatGPT for each element to create effective content that resonates with your audience.

1. **Understanding Your Audience** - The first and most crucial element of content creation is understanding your audience. Your content must be relevant and valuable to your target audience. Otherwise, it will not be

engaging for your audience. Therefore, you need to identify who your target audience is and what their needs and interests are. You can use tools like Google Analytics, social media analytics, and surveys to understand your audience better.

Once you understand your audience, you can create content that speaks directly to them. This step will help you build a relationship with them and establish yourself as an authority in your industry. Understanding your audience also means knowing which platforms they use to consume content. For example, if your audience is primarily on Instagram, you should focus on creating visual content such as images and videos.

Here are some ways you can use ChatGPT to understand your audience:

- **Conduct market research:** You can use Chat GPT to conduct market research by asking it questions about your target audience. For example, you can ask about your audience's interests, preferences, and pain points. This can help you create content that resonates with your audience.

- **Analyze social media conversations:** Chat GPT can be used to analyze social media conversations to understand what your audience is talking about. For example, you can ask it to analyze social media posts or comments to identify trends, topics, and keywords your audience is interested in.

- **Create customer personas:** You can use Chat GPT to create customer personas by asking it questions about your target audience. Customer personas can help you understand your audience's demographics, interests, and motivations and create content that meets their needs.

- **Conduct sentiment analysis:** You can use Chat GPT to conduct sentiment analysis to understand how your audience feels about your brand, products, or services. Sentiment analysis involves analyzing text to determine whether it is positive, negative, or neutral. This can help you create content that addresses your audience's concerns and preferences.

- **Use Chat GPT for content creativity:** You can use Chat GPT to generate content ideas that are tailored to your audience. For example, You can input keywords or topics relevant to your audience and let Chat GPT generate content ideas that are likely to resonate with them.

Overall, Chat GPT can be a powerful tool for understanding your audience and creating content that resonates with them. By leveraging its capabilities, you can gain insights into your audience's needs and preferences and create content that meets those needs.

2. **Identifying Your Goals** - Before you start creating content, you need to identify your goals. What do you want to achieve with your content? For example, do you want to drive more traffic to your website, generate leads, or increase brand awareness? Your content should align with your goals, and each piece should have a specific purpose.

Identifying your goals will also help you measure the success of your content. For example, you can use metrics like website traffic, engagement, and lead generation to determine how effectively your content achieves your goals.

ChatGPT can be a useful tool in identifying your goals in content creation. These are some ways you can use ChatGPT to identify your goals:

- **Ask for suggestions:** You can use ChatGPT for suggestions on your content goals. For example, you can ask it to suggest goals aligned with your business objectives. Then, based on your input, ChatGPT can suggest specific content goals relevant to your business.

- **Analyze competitor content:** You can use ChatGPT to analyze competitor content and identify goals that can help you differentiate your content. For example, you can ask it to analyze your competitor's content and suggest goals to help you create more engaging, informative, or entertaining content.

- **Conduct keyword research:** You can use ChatGPT to research keywords and identify goals that fit your audience's search intent. For example, you can input a keyword relevant to your business and ask ChatGPT to suggest content goals that can help you rank higher in search engine results pages.

- **Use ChatGPT for content creativity:** You can use ChatGPT to generate content ideas that are aligned with your content goals. For example, you can input a content goal and let ChatGPT generate content ideas that can help you achieve that goal.

- **Use ChatGPT for performance analysis:** You can use ChatGPT to analyze the performance of your existing content and identify goals that can help you improve your content strategy. For example, you can input a content piece and ask ChatGPT to analyze its performance based on engagement, traffic, and conversions. Based on the analysis, ChatGPT can suggest goals that can help you improve your content strategy.

ChatGPT is a powerful tool for identifying your goals in content creation. By utilizing its capabilities, you can gain insights into your business objectives, audience preferences, and content performance and create goals matching your business needs.

3. **Researching Your Topic -** The next step in content creation is researching your topic. You need to have a deep understanding of the topic you are writing about to provide value to your audience. Research can involve reading industry publications, reviewing case studies, conducting interviews, and more.

When researching your topic, it's important to stay up-to-date with the latest trends and news in your industry. This knowledge will help you create relevant and valuable content for your audience.

ChatGPT can be a useful tool for researching your topic in content creation. Here are some ways you can use ChatGPT to research your topic:

- **Generate keyword ideas:** ChatGPT can generate keyword ideas relevant to your topic. For example, you can input your topic and let ChatGPT generate a list of related keywords that you can use to optimize your content for search engines.

- **Find relevant sources:** You can use ChatGPT to find relevant sources to help you research your topic. For example, you can ask it to suggest articles, blog posts, or research papers relevant to your topic.

- **Conduct a literature review:** You can use ChatGPT to conduct a literature review of your topic. To do so, you input your topic and ask it to summarize the key findings of relevant research papers or articles.

- **Analyze social media conversations:** You can use ChatGPT to analyze social media conversations related to your topic. You can do that by asking it to analyze social media posts or comments to identify trends, topics, and keywords that are relevant to your topic.

- **Identify knowledge gaps:** You can use ChatGPT to identify knowledge gaps related to your topic. For example, you can input a question related to your topic and ask it to identify areas where more research is needed.

ChatGPT can make researching your topic an easy process. Using it; you can gain insights into your topic, identify relevant sources, fill knowledge gaps, and create informative and engaging content for your audience.

4. **Creating Engaging Headlines -** Your headline is the first thing your audience sees; it can make or break your content. Therefore, you need to create attention-grabbing headlines that will encourage your audience to click through to your content. Your headline should be concise and clear, and it should accurately reflect the content of your article.

One effective strategy for creating engaging headlines is to use numbers and statistics. For example, "10 Ways to Boost Your Website Traffic" is more compelling than "How to Boost Your Website Traffic."

ChatGPT can also help you in creating engaging headlines in content creation. Here are some ways you can use ChatGPT to create engaging headlines:

- **Generate headline ideas:** ChatGPT can generate headline ideas related to your content. For example, you can input your content topic and let ChatGPT generate a list of headline ideas relevant to your audience.

- **Analyze competitor headlines:** You can use ChatGPT to analyze your competitors' headlines and identify strategies to help you create more engaging headlines. To do so, you input your competitor's headline and ask ChatGPT to suggest improvements or variations to help you create a more compelling headline.

- **Conduct A/B testing:** You can use ChatGPT to conduct A/B testing of your headlines and identify the most effective headlines. You can do that by inputting two different headlines and asking ChatGPT to predict which one is more likely to generate engagement based on factors like click-through rates, social shares, or conversions.

- **Use ChatGPT for inspiration:** You can use ChatGPT for inspiration and creativity in creating engaging headlines. You tell it your content topic and ask it to suggest unconventional or creative headline ideas that can capture your audience's attention.

- **Use ChatGPT for optimization:** You can use ChatGPT to optimize your headlines for search engines or social media platforms. For example, you can input your headline and ask ChatGPT to suggest changes to improve its SEO or social media performance.

Chat GPT can be a powerful tool for creating engaging headlines in content creation. By leveraging its capabilities, you can generate headline ideas, analyze competitor strategies, conduct A/B testing, find inspiration, and optimize your headlines for maximum engagement.

5. **Writing Quality Content -** Once you have your topic and headline, it's time to start writing your content. Quality content is essential for

engaging your audience. Your content should be informative, well-researched, and provide value to your audience.

When writing your content, it's important to use language that is easy to understand. Avoid using jargon or technical terms that your audience may not be familiar with. In addition, your content should be organized and structured, with subheadings and bullet points to make it easy to read.

ChatGPT is a powerful tool that helps write quality content. Here are some ways you can use ChatGPT to write quality content:

- **Research topics:** You can use ChatGPT to research topics related to your content. For example, you can input a topic and let ChatGPT generate a list of related articles, blog posts, and research papers. This can help you gain insights into your topic, identify key points, and find supporting evidence for your arguments.

- **Generate outlines:** ChatGPT can generate outlines for your content. You can input your content idea and let ChatGPT generate a list of subtopics and headings to help structure your content. This can save you time and help you organize your thoughts more effectively.

- **Improve readability:** You can use ChatGPT to improve the readability of your content. To achieve that, you input your content and let ChatGPT suggest changes to make it more readable, such as simplifying complex sentences or removing unnecessary words. This can help you create content that is easy to understand and engaging for your audience.

- **Check grammar and spelling:** You can use ChatGPT to check the grammar and spelling of your content. To do so, you can input your content and let ChatGPT identify any errors or mistakes that you may have missed. This will help you create content that is free of errors and professional-looking.

- **Generate summaries:** You can use ChatGPT to generate summaries of your content. For example, you can input your content and let ChatGPT generate a summary highlighting the key points and takeaways. This can help you create content that is easy to digest and shareable on social media.

ChatGPT is a versatile tool that can be used in various stages of the content creation process. By leveraging its capabilities, you can generate content ideas, research topics, create outlines, improve readability, check grammar and spelling, and generate summaries. This can help you create quality content that is informative, engaging, and valuable to your target audience.

6. **Using Visuals** - Visuals are a crucial element of content creation. They can help break up text and make your content more engaging. They can include images, infographics, videos, and more. When choosing visuals, it's important to use high-quality images and graphics that are relevant to your content.

Visuals can also help communicate complex information in a more accessible way. For example, an infographic can effectively present data or statistics in a visually appealing format.

While Chat GPT is not specifically designed for creating visuals, there are several ways it can be used to support visual content creation:

- **Generate ideas for visual content:** You can use ChatGPT to generate ideas for visual content that align with your written content. For example, you can input a topic or keyword and ask ChatGPT to suggest images, infographics, or videos that are relevant to your content.

- **Provide inspiration for the visual design:** You can use ChatGPT to provide inspiration for the visual design of your content. For example, you can input a description of your brand or content style and ask ChatGPT to suggest visual design elements that align with your brand or style.

- **Automate the creation of simple visuals:** ChatGPT can create simple visuals like charts, graphs, and diagrams. You can input data and ask ChatGPT to represent that data visually.

- **Provide insights for creating visuals:** ChatGPT can be used to provide insights for creating visuals. For example, you can input a description of your audience or content and ask ChatGPT to suggest visual elements more likely to engage your audience.

- **Support the creation of multimedia content:** ChatGPT can be used to support the creation of multimedia content. For example, you can input an audio or video file and ask ChatGPT to generate captions, transcripts, or descriptions that can be used as text content.

- **Create mockups and prototypes:** ChatGPT can create mockups and prototypes for visual content. For example, you can input a description of a visual element and ask ChatGPT to generate a rough sketch or prototype of that element.

Overall, while ChatGPT is not specifically designed for creating visuals, it can be a useful tool for creating visual content by generating ideas, providing inspiration, automating simple visual creation, providing insights, supporting multimedia content, and creating mockups and prototypes.

7. **Promoting Your Content -** Creating great content is only half the battle. You also need to promote your content so that your audience can find it. There are several ways to promote your content, including:

a. Social Media Marketing - Social media is one of the most effective ways to promote your content. You can share your content on social media platforms like Facebook, Twitter, and LinkedIn and encourage your followers to share it with their network.

b. Email Marketing - Email marketing is another effective way to promote your content. You can send your content to your email list and encourage them to read and share it. You can also use email automation to automatically send your content to new subscribers.

c. **Influencer Marketing** - Influencer marketing involves partnering with influencers in your industry to promote your content. Influencers have a large following and can help you reach a wider audience. You can offer them incentives such as free products or services to promote your content.

d. **Search Engine Optimization** - Search engine optimization (SEO) involves optimizing your content for search engines like Google. This approach can help your content rank higher in search engine results pages, making it easier for your audience to find. SEO involves using keywords, meta descriptions, and other tactics to improve your content's visibility.

e. **Paid Advertising** - Paid advertising can help promote your content to a wider audience. You can use platforms like Google Ads and Facebook Ads to target specific demographics and reach people who may be interested in your content.

f. **Content Syndication** - Content syndication involves publishing your content on other websites or platforms. This can help you reach a wider audience and drive more traffic to your website. For example, you can syndicate your content using platforms like Outbrain or Taboola.

Promoting your content is one of the most important elements in the content generation field because it allows you to monetize your content by reaching your target audience. ChatGPT can support the promotion of your content by providing insights and suggestions for various promotional activities. Here are some ways you can use ChatGPT to promote your content:

- **Social media promotion:** ChatGPT can be used to generate social media posts that promote your content. For example, you can input your content and ask ChatGPT to suggest social media posts to promote it. This can help you generate engaging posts that are tailored to your audience.

- **Email marketing:** ChatGPT can be used to generate email marketing campaigns that promote your content. For example, you can input your content and ask ChatGPT to suggest email campaigns to promote it. This can help you create targeted campaigns more likely to engage your subscribers.

- **Influencer marketing:** ChatGPT can be used to identify potential influencers who can promote your content. It can suggest influencers who have previously promoted similar content or have an audience that aligns with your target audience. This can help you identify potential partners for influencer marketing campaigns.

- **Content syndication:** ChatGPT can be used to suggest websites or blogs where you can syndicate your content. By analyzing your input, it can suggest websites or blogs that are relevant to your content and have a large audience. This can help you reach a wider audience and generate more traffic to your website.

- **Paid advertising:** ChatGPT can be used to suggest paid advertising campaigns that promote your content. For example, you can input your content and ask ChatGPT to suggest paid advertising campaigns relevant to your content and target audience. This can help you create targeted campaigns more likely to generate traffic and conversions.

- **Content repurposing:** ChatGPT can suggest ways to repurpose your content for different platforms or media. This can help you create new content that is tailored to different platforms and media.

- **SEO optimization:** ChatGPT can be used to suggest ways to optimize your content for search engines. It suggests keywords, meta descriptions, or titles that can improve your content's ranking on search engines by analyzing your content. This can help you generate more organic traffic to your website.

EXAMPLE:

INPUT: SEO Keyword recommendations for a blog about ChatGPT

OUTPUT: Here are some SEO keyword recommendations for a blog about ChatGPT:

1. **ChatGPT:** This is the main keyword that should be included throughout the blog to ensure that the content is relevant to the topic.

2. **Artificial Intelligence:** ChatGPT is an AI-based language model, so including this keyword can help attract readers interested in AI and its applications.

3. **Natural Language Processing:** This is another relevant keyword that can be included in the blog to describe the technology behind ChatGPT.

4. **Content Creation:** ChatGPT can be used for content creation, so including this keyword can help attract readers interested in using AI for content creation.

5. **Language Model:** ChatGPT is a language model, so including this keyword can attract readers interested in language models and their applications.

6. **Machine Learning:** ChatGPT uses machine learning algorithms, so including this keyword can help attract readers interested in machine learning and its applications.

7. **Writing Assistant:** ChatGPT can be used as a writing assistant, so including this keyword can help attract readers looking for writing tools and resources.

8. **Natural Language Generation:** This is another relevant keyword that can be included in the blog to describe the technology behind ChatGPT and its applications for natural language generation.

ChatGPT can be a useful tool to promote your content by providing insights and suggestions for various promotional activities, such as social media promotion, email marketing, influencer marketing, content syndication, paid advertising, content repurposing, and SEO optimization. By leveraging its capabilities, you can create engaging and targeted promotional campaigns tailored to your audience and generate more traffic and conversions to your website.

You can use this workflow tool to help ease the content creation process.

Step 1: Keyword Tool – First, you need to determine the keywords you need to use for your blog, depending on the topic you plan to write. Keyword tools are online applications or software programs that help users research and identify the best keywords to optimize their content for search engines.

Topic Clusters – After getting your keywords, note that some of them might be redundant. So, you need to add them to topic clusters. Topic clusters refer to a content strategy that organizes content around a central topic or theme, with multiple subtopics or related keywords that support and link to the central topic. This strategy helps to improve the overall relevance and authority of a website or blog by creating a network of interlinked content.

Jasper + ChatGPT – Next, you can write your content through Jasper or ChatGPT. ChatGPT can be used to write content. It is an artificial intelligence language model trained on a large corpus of text data, allowing it to generate human-like text based on a given prompt or topic. Jasper Chat is a chatbot development platform that allows businesses to build and deploy chatbots across various channels such as Facebook Messenger, WhatsApp, and websites. It provides a drag-and-drop interface for creating chatbots and a library of pre-built templates and integrations with other software applications.

Surfer SEO (Optimize) – In this stage, you need to optimize your blog's keywords to ensure they are properly placed and incorporated into your output. You can use platforms like Surfer SEO, a search engine optimization (SEO) tool that helps businesses optimize their content and improve their website's ranking in search engine results pages (SERPs). It provides various features to help users optimize on-page, including content analysis, keyword research, and website audits.

Grammarly or Quillbot – Next, check your grammar through Grammarly, an online writing tool that uses artificial intelligence (AI) to help users improve their grammar, spelling, punctuation, and writing style. It is available as a browser extension for Chrome, Firefox, Safari, and Edge, as well as a standalone web application and a desktop app. You can also use Quillbot to better your writing. It is an AI-based writing tool with various features to help users improve their writing. For example, it can be used for paraphrasing, summarizing, and generating content from scratch. Quillbot uses natural language processing (NLP) technology to analyze text and suggest improvements based on context, grammar, and style.

Creating images through AI is a technique that involves using artificial intelligence (AI) algorithms to generate images from scratch or modify existing images.

Rank Math – Next, run it through Rank Math, a search engine optimization (SEO) plugin for WordPress websites that helps users optimize their website content for search engines. It provides various features to improve on-page SEO, including keyword optimization, site analysis, and content optimization suggestions.

SEO processes – This includes social sharing and generating traffic to your blog. SEO (Search Engine Optimization) is the process of optimizing a website to rank higher in search engine results pages (SERPs) and increase organic traffic to the site.

In summary, by following these elements, you can create effective content that resonates with your audience and helps you achieve your business goals.

RESEARCH ASSISTANCE

Aside from content creation, ChatGPT can also be used for research assistance. Research is the process of gathering and analyzing information or data to discover new knowledge or better understand a particular topic or phenomenon. It involves a systematic approach to collecting and evaluating information from various sources, including books, academic journals, online databases, interviews, surveys, and experiments.

Research assistance refers to the support and guidance individuals or services provide to help researchers navigate the research process. Research assistants are individuals trained to support researchers in different ways, such as helping with literature reviews, conducting surveys or interviews, analyzing data, and providing feedback on research proposals or manuscripts.

Services such as libraries, online databases, or research centers can also provide research assistance. These services can offer resources such as access to academic journals, online research tools, and expert advice on conducting research in a particular field.

Research assistance is an essential component of the research process. It involves providing support and guidance to researchers throughout their research projects. Several elements make up effective research assistance, including:

1. **Access to resources:** One of the most important elements of research assistance is providing access to resources that researchers need to conduct their research effectively, including academic journals, online databases, books, and other research materials.

ChatGPT is a useful tool for accessing resources for research assistance. Here are some ways you can use ChatGPT to access resources:

- **Ask for recommendations:** You can ask ChatGPT for recommendations on research materials in your field of study. ChatGPT can provide you with a list of resources that you can use to conduct your research.

- **Search for articles:** You can ask ChatGPT for articles on specific topics or keywords. It can provide you with a list of relevant articles that you can use in your literature review.

- **Access open-access resources:** You can ask ChatGPT for open-access resources such as open-access journals, free online databases, and public domain books. ChatGPT can provide you with a list of resources you can access without paying for them.

- **Obtain research papers:** You can ask ChatGPT to locate research papers on specific topics or keywords. It can provide you with links to papers that you can use in your literature review or as references in your research.

- **Get guidance on research methods:** You can ask ChatGPT for guidance on research methods and techniques. It can provide information on the different research methods and techniques commonly used in your field of study.

- **Obtain information on research ethics:** You can ask ChatGPT for information on research ethics guidelines and best practices. ChatGPT can provide you with information on the ethical considerations you need to consider when conducting your research.

- **Access research tools and software:** You can ask ChatGPT for recommendations on tools and software to help you conduct your research more effectively. ChatGPT can provide information on tools and software used in your field of study.

To use ChatGPT to access research assistance resources, you need to be specific in your requests and provide as much information as possible, which will help ChatGPT to provide you with more accurate and relevant information. Additionally, it's important to verify the information provided by ChatGPT and conduct your research to ensure that the resources and information provided are reliable and relevant to your specific research project.

2. **Expertise:** Research assistants should have expertise in their field's research methods and techniques. This includes knowledge of quantitative and qualitative research methods, statistical analysis, data management, and research ethics. They should also be able to provide guidance on the best practices for conducting research and be able to help researchers navigate the research process.

ChatGPT can help you gain expertise in a field of study with its research assistance abilities. Here are some ways you can use ChatGPT to gain expertise:

- **Ask for general information:** You can ask ChatGPT about a field of study or a specific topic within that field. ChatGPT can provide you with an overview of the field and its sub-disciplines, key concepts and theories, and historical developments.

- **Ask for specific information:** You can ask ChatGPT for specific information about a topic or concept you need to be explained. ChatGPT can provide detailed explanations, definitions, and examples to help you understand the topic better.

- **Ask for recommendations:** You can ask ChatGPT for recommendations on books, journals, articles, and other resources that can help you gain expertise in your field of study.

- **Get guidance on research methods:** You can ask ChatGPT for guidance on research methods and techniques commonly used in your field. It can provide information on the different research methods and techniques and their advantages and disadvantages.

- **Request for examples:** You can ask ChatGPT for examples of research studies or experiments. ChatGPT can provide examples of research studies or experiments that can help you better understand how to design and conduct research in your field.

- **Ask for expert opinions:** You can ask ChatGPT for expert opinions on specific topics or concepts within your field of study. ChatGPT can provide insights from experts in your field that can help you better understand the topic.

It's important to be specific in your requests and provide as much information as possible when using ChatGPT. This will help ChatGPT to provide you with more accurate and relevant information.

3. **Assistance with literature reviews:** A literature review is an important part of the research process, as it gives an overview and analysis of existing research on a specific topic. Research assistants can help researchers identify and access relevant literature, as well as help them organize and synthesize the information they find. They can also help researchers identify gaps in the literature and suggest areas for further research.

ChatGPT can be a useful tool for generating literature reviews for research assistance. Here are some steps to follow:

- **Define your research question:** Before generating a literature review, define your research question or topic. This will help you focus your search and ensure that the literature you gather is relevant to your research.

- **Identify keywords and search terms:** Once you have defined your research question or topic, you need to identify keywords and search terms relevant to your research. You can ask ChatGPT for suggestions on relevant keywords and search terms.

- **Conduct a search:** Using the keywords and search terms, conduct a search of academic databases, such as JSTOR, Google Scholar, or

PubMed, to find relevant literature. You can ask ChatGPT to suggest academic databases relevant to your research topic.

- **Filter and select relevant literature:** Once you have done your search, you must filter and select relevant literature based on your research question or topic. You can ask ChatGPT to help you filter and select relevant literature based on your search terms and research question.

- **Organize and summarize the literature:** Once you have gathered relevant literature, you need to organize and summarize it meaningfully. You can ask ChatGPT to help you organize and summarize the literature based on key themes or concepts.

- **Analyze and synthesize the literature:** Once you have organized and summarized it, you need to analyze and synthesize the literature to provide insights and conclusions about your research topic. You can ask ChatGPT to help you analyze and synthesize the literature based on your research question.

- **Write the literature review:** Once you have analyzed and synthesized the literature, you need to write the literature review. You can ask ChatGPT to help you write the literature review based on the literature's organization, summary, analysis, and synthesis.

It's important to note that while ChatGPT can be a useful tool for generating literature reviews, it's important to verify the information provided and conduct your own research to ensure that the literature review is accurate and relevant to your specific research project. Additionally, it's important to follow the guidelines and requirements of your research project or institution when writing a literature review.

4. **Data collection and analysis:** Research assistants can help researchers with data collection and analysis. They help with surveys, interviews, and experiments, as well as with data entry, cleaning, and analysis.

Research assistants should be knowledgeable about the data collection and analysis tools and techniques used in their field of study.

ChatGPT can be a useful tool for generating ideas and approaches for data collection and analysis in research. Here are some steps to follow:

- **Define your research question:** Before generating data collection and analysis strategies, you need to define your research question or topic.

- **Identify relevant variables:** Once you have defined your research question or topic, identify relevant variables or factors that may impact your research. You can ask ChatGPT to suggest variables or factors relevant to your research topic.

- **Identify data collection methods:** Once you have identified relevant variables, you need to identify appropriate data collection methods for your research. You can ask ChatGPT to suggest data collection methods relevant to your research topic.

- **Develop data collection instruments:** Once you have identified data collection methods, you need to develop data collection instruments, such as surveys, questionnaires, or interviews. You can ask ChatGPT to suggest questions or prompts connected to your research topic.

- **Collect data:** Once you have developed data collection instruments, you need to collect data. You can ask ChatGPT to suggest ways to collect data, such as through online surveys or in-person interviews.

- **Analyze data:** Once you have collected data, you need to analyze it to draw insights and conclusions about your research. Again, you can ask ChatGPT to suggest appropriate data analysis methods for your research topic.

- **Interpret results:** Once you have analyzed data, you must interpret the results to conclude your research. You can ask ChatGPT to suggest ways to interpret the results, such as by creating charts or graphs to visualize data trends.

5. **Feedback on research** proposals and manuscripts: Research assistants can provide feedback on research proposals and manuscripts. They help review proposals and manuscripts for clarity, coherence, and compliance with research ethics guidelines. They can also provide feedback on the research design, methodology, and analysis and suggest areas for improvement.

Getting feedback on research proposals and manuscripts is an important part of the research process. ChatGPT can be useful for generating feedback on your research proposals and manuscripts. Here are some steps to follow:

- **Define the purpose of your research:** Before seeking feedback, you need to define the purpose of your research clearly. Then, you can ask ChatGPT to suggest questions to help you refine the purpose of your research.

- **Identify the key elements of your research proposal or manuscript:** Once you have defined the purpose of your research, you need to identify the key elements of your research proposal or manuscript. These may include the introduction, literature review, methods, results, and conclusion. You can ask ChatGPT to suggest questions to help you identify the key elements of your research proposal or manuscript.

- **Ask ChatGPT to review your research proposal or manuscript:** Once you have identified the key elements of your research proposal or manuscript, you can ask ChatGPT to review it. ChatGPT can provide feedback on your research proposal or manuscript's clarity, organization, and logic.

- **Revise your research proposal or manuscript based on feedback:** Once you have received feedback from ChatGPT, you can revise your research proposal or manuscript based on the feedback. You can ask

ChatGPT to suggest revisions or improvements to your research proposal or manuscript.

- **Get feedback from human experts:** While ChatGPT can be a useful tool for generating feedback, it's important also to seek feedback from human experts in your field. ChatGPT can suggest resources or experts who can provide feedback on your research proposal or manuscript.

- **Incorporate feedback from human experts:** Once you have received feedback from human experts, you can incorporate the feedback into your research proposal or manuscript. You can ask ChatGPT to suggest ways to incorporate feedback into your research proposal or manuscript.

It's important to note that while ChatGPT can be a useful tool for generating feedback on research proposals and manuscripts, it's important to verify the feedback provided and to seek feedback from human experts in your field.

6. **Collaboration and communication:** Research assistants should be able to collaborate effectively with researchers and communicate clearly and professionally. This entails promptly responding to emails and other communications, attending meetings and providing updates on the research progress, and working collaboratively with researchers to achieve research goals.

Collaboration and communication are essential components of research. ChatGPT can be a useful tool for facilitating collaboration and communication among researchers. Here are some ways to use ChatGPT for collaboration and communication in research:

- **Brainstorming ideas:** ChatGPT can suggest questions to help you brainstorm ideas and suggest potential research topics.

- **Sharing and discussing research:** You can use ChatGPT to suggest discussion topics or generate questions to facilitate research discussion.

- **Collaborative writing:** You can use ChatGPT to suggest writing ideas or generate questions to facilitate the writing process.

- **Project management:** ChatGPT can suggest project timelines or general questions to help manage the project.

- **Collaboration with international researchers:** ChatGPT can be particularly useful for facilitating collaboration with international researchers. You can use ChatGPT to suggest questions to facilitate communication or to provide translations for communication with non-native English speakers.

- **Conflict resolution:** ChatGPT can be used to resolve conflicts that may arise during the research process by suggesting questions or strategies for resolving conflicts among researchers.

- **Scheduling and planning meetings:** ChatGPT can be used to schedule and plan meetings among researchers. You can use ChatGPT to suggest meeting times or to generate questions to help plan the meeting agenda.

ChatGPT can be a useful tool for facilitating collaboration and communication among researchers. However, it is important to remember that ChatGPT is a machine-learning model that can only partially replace human communication and collaboration. Therefore, it is also important to have regular communication and collaboration with other researchers in person or through other communication tools.

7. **Ethical considerations:** Research assistants should be knowledgeable about research ethics and be able to guide ethical considerations in research. This includes ensuring that research is conducted ethically, protecting the confidentiality of research participants, and obtaining informed consent from research participants.

When conducting research, it is important to consider the ethical implications of your work. ChatGPT can be used to generate ethical considerations for research projects in several ways:

- **Suggesting relevant ethical guidelines:** ChatGPT can be used to suggest relevant ethical guidelines for your research project. For example, if you are conducting research with human subjects, ChatGPT can suggest guidelines from organizations such as the Institutional Review Board (IRB) or the Declaration of Helsinki.

- **Identifying potential ethical concerns:** ChatGPT can help you identify potential ethical concerns related to your research project. For example, if you are conducting research with vulnerable populations, ChatGPT can suggest potential ethical concerns related to informed consent, confidentiality, and potential harm.

- **Offering suggestions for ethical solutions:** ChatGPT can provide suggestions for ethical solutions to potential concerns. For example, if you are conducting research with vulnerable populations, ChatGPT can suggest strategies for obtaining informed consent, maintaining confidentiality, and minimizing potential harm.

- **Identifying potential biases:** ChatGPT can help you identify potential biases in your research design or analysis that may have ethical implications. For example, if you are researching a sensitive topic, ChatGPT can suggest potential biases related to cultural or societal norms that may influence the research findings.

- **Offering suggestions for addressing biases:** ChatGPT can provide suggestions for addressing potential biases in your research. For example, if you are researching a sensitive topic, ChatGPT can suggest strategies for minimizing the influence of cultural or societal norms on the research findings.

- **Providing resources for ethical considerations:** ChatGPT can suggest resources for addressing ethical considerations in your research project. For example, ChatGPT can suggest relevant articles, books, or guidelines for ethical considerations in your field of study.

While ChatGPT can be a useful tool for generating ethical considerations in research projects, it is important to consult with experts in your field and obtain appropriate training in research ethics.

8. **Time management:** Research assistants should be skilled in time management and be able to manage their time effectively to meet project deadlines. This includes prioritizing tasks, creating timelines, and ensuring timely project deliverables.

Time management is a critical aspect of conducting research. ChatGPT can be used to provide suggestions and insights on time management for research assistance in many ways:

- **Developing a research schedule:** ChatGPT can be used to develop a research schedule that outlines the tasks and milestones that need to be completed throughout the project. In addition, ChatGPT can suggest appropriate timelines for each task and help identify potential roadblocks or bottlenecks.

- **Time estimation for tasks:** ChatGPT can estimate the time required for specific tasks. For example, ChatGPT can estimate the time required to conduct a literature review or analyze data.

- **Prioritizing tasks:** ChatGPT can help prioritize tasks by providing insights into which tasks are most critical for the project's success. ChatGPT can also suggest strategies for completing high-priority tasks efficiently.

- **Identifying time-saving strategies:** ChatGPT can help identify time-saving strategies for specific tasks. For example, ChatGPT can suggest software tools to automate data analysis or streamline the literature review process.

- **Creating a work-life balance:** ChatGPT can also suggest strategies for creating a work-life balance when conducting research. For example,

ChatGPT can suggest ways to manage stress and maintain a healthy lifestyle.

- **Managing procrastination:** ChatGPT can provide strategies for managing procrastination and staying on track with the research schedule. For example, ChatGPT can suggest strategies for breaking down large tasks into smaller, more manageable ones or setting realistic goals.

ChatGPT can be a useful tool for managing time when conducting research. However, it is important to remember that ChatGPT is a machine-learning model that can only partially replace human judgment or time management skills. Therefore, consulting with experts in your field and obtaining appropriate training in time management and project management is important.

9. **Professional development:** Research assistants should be committed to ongoing professional development and be willing to learn new skills and techniques to enhance their effectiveness as research assistants. This includes attending training sessions, workshops, and conferences and seeking feedback and mentorship from more experienced researchers.

Professional development is an important aspect of research assistance as it helps individuals to develop the skills and knowledge required to succeed in their field. ChatGPT can be used to provide suggestions and insights on professional development for research assistance in several ways:

- **Identifying relevant training programs:** ChatGPT can help identify relevant training programs that can help individuals develop their skills and knowledge in their field. For example, ChatGPT can suggest online courses or workshops covering research methods, data analysis, and scientific writing.

- **Providing insights into emerging trends and technologies:** ChatGPT can provide insights into emerging trends and technologies in a particular field of study. For example, ChatGPT can suggest new research methods or technologies being used in a particular area of research.

- **Helping individuals to stay up-to-date with current research:** ChatGPT can help individuals stay up-to-date with current research by suggesting relevant articles, journals, and conference proceedings.

- **Providing insights into career development:** ChatGPT can provide insights into career development by suggesting strategies for career advancement or identifying opportunities for professional growth. For example, ChatGPT can suggest networking events or conferences where individuals can connect with other researchers in their field.

- **Providing guidance on publishing research:** ChatGPT can provide guidance on publishing research by suggesting appropriate journals and providing tips for writing and submitting manuscripts.

- **Offering mentorship and guidance:** ChatGPT can also provide mentorship and guidance to individuals just starting in their field. For example, ChatGPT can suggest strategies for building a strong academic network or provide advice on how to approach a difficult research problem.

ChatGPT can be a useful tool for professional development in research assistance. However, It is important also to seek guidance from experts in your field and obtain appropriate training to develop your skills and knowledge in research assistance.

Research assistance is an important component of the research process that involves supporting and guiding researchers. Effective research assistance involves providing access to resources, expertise in research methods and techniques, assistance with literature review, data collection, and analysis, feedback on research proposals and manuscripts, collaboration and communication, knowledge of ethical considerations, time management skills, and a commitment to ongoing professional development.

LANGUAGE LEARNING (INCLUDING COMPUTER LANGUAGES CODING)

Language learning is acquiring a new language, which involves developing listening, speaking, reading, and writing skills. It is a complex and ongoing process that requires significant time and effort to master.

Language learning can take many forms, including formal classroom instruction, self-study through textbooks and language learning software, immersion programs, and language exchange programs. The method used for language learning will depend on the individual's learning style, the resources available, and their language learning goals.

Learning a new language can provide many benefits, including improved communication skills, increased cultural understanding and awareness, and enhanced job opportunities. It can also promote cognitive development and improve memory and problem-solving skills.

However, language learning can also be challenging, requiring dedication and persistenceTherefore, it is important to set realistic goals and to practice regularly to make progress in language learning.

Learning a new language could also mean computer language coding. Computer languages or coding languages are a set of rules and instructions that a computer can understand and execute. They are used to create software applications, websites, and other digital products. Here are some of the most common coding languages:

1. **HTML/CSS:** HTML (Hypertext Markup Language) and CSS (Cascading Style Sheets) are used for building websites. HTML

provides the website's structure, while CSS is used for styling and design.

2. **JavaScript:** JavaScript is a dynamic programming language used for creating interactive and dynamic web pages. It is also used for building web applications, games, and mobile apps.

3. **Python:** Python is a high-level programming language that is easy to learn and understand. It is widely used in scientific computing, data analysis, web development, and artificial intelligence.

4. **Java:** Java is a popular programming language used for developing enterprise-level applications, mobile apps, and games.

5. **C++:** C++ is a powerful programming language for building system software, operating systems, and games.

6. **Ruby:** Ruby is a high-level programming language that is easy to read and write. It is used for building web applications, web servers, and scripting.

7. **Swift:** Swift is a programming language developed by Apple for developing iOS and macOS applications.

Learning a coding language requires dedication and practice. Starting with a language that aligns with your learning goals and interests is essential. Many online resources, tutorials, and courses are available to learn coding languages, and ChatGPT can also assist in answering any questions you may have.

Language learning is a complex process that involves several elements. Here are some of the key elements of language learning and how ChatGPT can help you with each element:

1. **Vocabulary:** Vocabulary refers to the words and phrases used in a language. Learning vocabulary is essential for effective communication in a language.

Here are some ways to use ChatGPT to learn new vocabulary:

- **Generating flashcards:** Flashcards are a great way to learn and memorize vocabulary. You can use ChatGPT to generate flashcards with new vocabulary words and their translations. You can also add images or audio files to the flashcards to help you remember the words better.

- **Practicing using new vocabulary:** You can use ChatGPT to practice using new vocabulary words in context. For example, you can ask ChatGPT to generate sentences using a new word you just learned or ask for a word's definition in the context of a particular sentence.

- **Quizzing yourself:** You can use ChatGPT to quiz yourself on the new vocabulary you have learned. For example, you can ask ChatGPT to generate a list of vocabulary words and their translations and then quiz yourself by trying to recall them from memory.

- **Practicing pronunciation:** ChatGPT can also help you practice pronouncing new vocabulary words. For example, you can ask ChatGPT to generate audio recordings of words or sentences and then practice repeating them until you pronounce them correctly.

2. **Grammar:** Grammar refers to the rules that govern the structure of a language. Learning grammar is important for understanding the logic and syntax of a language.

ChatGPT can be a helpful tool for learning grammar in a new language. Here are some tips on how to use ChatGPT for this purpose:

- **Ask ChatGPT to explain grammar rules:** ChatGPT can help explain grammar rules in a new language. For example, you can ask it to explain a specific rule or ask for an overview of the grammar of a particular language.

- **Practice grammar exercises:** You can ask ChatGPT to generate grammar exercises for you to practice. For example, you can ask for exercises on verb conjugation, sentence structure, or noun declension.

- **Ask ChatGPT to correct your sentences:** You can practice your grammar by asking ChatGPT to correct your sentences.

- **Use ChatGPT to check your writing:** You can use ChatGPT to check your writing for grammar errors. For example, you can ask ChatGPT to review an essay or email you wrote in a new language, and it can identify any grammatical errors you made.

- **Use ChatGPT to practice conversation:** ChatGPT can also help you practice using grammar in conversation. For example, you can ask ChatGPT to generate conversation prompts and then practice using grammar rules in your responses.

Chat GPT can be a helpful tool for learning grammar in a new language. However, it is important to supplement this with other language learning methods, such as immersion, speaking practice, and vocabulary study, to master a language fully.

3. **Pronunciation:** Pronunciation refers to the correct way of saying words and sounds in a language. Learning correct pronunciation is essential for clear and effective communication in a language.

ChatGPT can be a useful tool for learning pronunciation in several ways:

1. **Practice reading out loud:** You can input text into ChatGPT and then read the output out loud to practice your pronunciation. ChatGPT can provide feedback on whether you are pronouncing words correctly, and you can use this feedback to improve your pronunciation.

2. **Listen to ChatGPT's pronunciation:** ChatGPT can also pronounce words for you, so you can listen to its pronunciation and compare it to your own. This can help you identify areas where you need to improve your pronunciation.

3. **Ask ChatGPT for pronunciation tips:** You can ask ChatGPT specific questions about pronouncing certain words or sounds. Then, ChatGPT

can provide you with tips and examples to help you improve your pronunciation.

Here are some examples of how you can use ChatGPT to improve your pronunciation:

Example 1: Input: "The quick brown fox jumps over the lazy dog." Output: "The kwik braun foks jumps ovr the lezi dog."

Practice reading the output out loud, and compare your pronunciation to ChatGPT's. Then, focus on the areas where your pronunciation differs from ChatGPT's and work on improving those sounds.

Example 2: Input: "How do you pronounce 'pronunciation'?" Output: "prəˌnʌnsiˈeɪʃən"

Listen to ChatGPT's pronunciation and repeat it out loud. Pay attention to the stress and intonation of the word, as well as the individual sounds.

Example 3: Input: "Can you give me some tips on how to pronounce 'th' correctly?" Output: "To produce the 'th' sound, place your tongue between your teeth and blow air out gently. The sound is made with the tip of your tongue and the top front teeth."

Use ChatGPT's tips to practice pronouncing the 'th' sound correctly. Then, repeat the sound several times until you feel comfortable with it.

4. **Listening comprehension:** Listening comprehension refers to the ability to understand spoken language. It is important for effective communication and comprehension of a language.

ChatGPT can be used to improve your listening comprehension in a few ways:

● **Listening to spoken text:** You can input spoken text into ChatGPT and listen to its output to practice your listening comprehension skills. ChatGPT can also provide a transcript of the spoken text, so you can read along and check your understanding.

- **Asking for clarification:** If you don't understand something that ChatGPT says, you can ask it to clarify or repeat it. This can help you improve your ability to understand spoken language.

- **Practicing with different accents:** ChatGPT can simulate different accents and dialects, which can help you improve your ability to understand different types of spoken language.

Here are some examples of how you can use ChatGPT to improve your listening comprehension:

Example 1: Input: "Can you read this passage out loud for me?" Output: ChatGPT reads the passage out loud.

Listen to ChatGPT's reading of the passage and try to understand as much as possible. If there are parts you don't understand, use the transcript to read along and check your understanding.

Example 2: Input: "Can you repeat that, please?" Output: ChatGPT repeats its previous statement.

If you need help understanding what ChatGPT said, ask it to repeat what it said. This can help you catch any words or phrases that you may have missed the first time.

Example 3: Input: "Can you speak with a British accent?" Output: ChatGPT speaks with a British accent.

Listening to ChatGPT speak with a different accent can help you improve your understanding of different types of spoken language. Try to listen for differences in pronunciation, intonation, and vocabulary.

5. **Reading comprehension:** Reading comprehension refers to the ability to understand written language. It is important for understanding written materials, such as books, articles, and other texts.

ChatGPT can be a useful tool for improving your reading comprehension in a few ways:

- **Summarizing text:** You can input text into ChatGPT and ask it to summarize the text's main points. This can help you identify the most important information and improve your understanding of the text.

- **Defining unfamiliar words:** If you encounter an unfamiliar word while reading, you can input it into ChatGPT and ask for a definition. This can help you better understand the word's meaning and how it is used in the text.

- **Asking for clarification:** If you come across a confusing sentence or paragraph, you can input it into ChatGPT and ask for clarification. ChatGPT can provide explanations or examples to help you better understand the text.

Here are some examples of how you can use ChatGPT to improve your reading comprehension:

Example 1: Input: "Can you summarize this article for me?" Output: ChatGPT provides a summary of the article.

Read ChatGPT's article summary and compare it to your own understanding of the text. Then, if there are any differences, re-read the article to clarify your understanding.

Example 2: Input: "What does 'ubiquitous' mean?" Output: ChatGPT defines the word.

If you encounter an unfamiliar word, input it into ChatGPT and ask for a definition. This can help you better understand the word's meaning and how it is used in the text.

Example 3: Input: "Can you explain what this sentence means?" Output: ChatGPT provides an explanation of the sentence.

6. **Writing skills:** Writing skills refer to the ability to write effectively in a language. It is important for communicating ideas and thoughts in written form.

ChatGPT can be a useful tool for improving your writing skills in different ways:

- **Generating ideas:** You can input a topic into ChatGPT and ask it to generate ideas for your writing. ChatGPT can provide suggestions for arguments, examples, and supporting evidence to help you develop your ideas.

- **Checking grammar and spelling:** ChatGPT can also check your grammar and spelling as you write. This can help you avoid common errors and improve the overall quality of your writing.

- **Providing feedback:** You can input your writing into ChatGPT and ask for feedback on the structure, coherence, and clarity of your writing. ChatGPT can also suggest changes and improvements to help you refine your writing skills.

Here are some examples of how you can use ChatGPT to improve your writing skills:

Example 1: Input: "I need some ideas for a persuasive essay on climate change." Output: ChatGPT provides several ideas and arguments for the essay.

Use ChatGPT's suggestions to develop your ideas for the essay. These suggestions can help you structure your argument and provide supporting evidence to support your claims.

Example 2: Input: "Can you check my grammar and spelling in this paragraph?" Output: ChatGPT provides feedback on the paragraph, highlighting any errors.

Example 3: Input: "Can you give me feedback on the structure of my essay?" Output: ChatGPT provides suggestions for improving the structure and coherence of the essay.

Use ChatGPT's feedback to refine the structure and coherence of your essay. In addition, this feedback can help you to create a clear and well-organized piece of writing that effectively communicates your ideas to the reader.

These elements are interconnected and complement each other, and they should all be given due attention in the language learning process.

How to Use Chat GPT in Learning Computer Language Coding

ChatGPT can be a helpful tool for learning computer coding languages; it helps with the following:

1. **Providing examples:** You can input a coding concept or problem into ChatGPT and ask for an example of how to write the code to solve it. In addition, ChatGPT can provide sample code snippets that you can study and learn from.

2. **Explaining concepts:** You can input a coding concept or term into ChatGPT and ask for an explanation. ChatGPT can provide a clear and concise explanation of the concept or term to help you understand it better.

3. **Troubleshooting:** You can input a coding error message into ChatGPT and ask for help troubleshooting the issue. ChatGPT can provide suggestions for identifying and resolving the error.

Here are some examples of how you can use ChatGPT to learn computer coding languages:

Example 1: Input: "Can you show me an example of how to create a for loop in Python?" Output: ChatGPT provides a code snippet demonstrating how to create a for loop in Python.

Study the code snippet provided by ChatGPT to understand how to create a for loop in Python. You can modify the code and experiment with different values to understand how it works.

Example 2: Input: "What is the difference between an array and a linked list in Java?" Output: ChatGPT provides an explanation of the differences between an array and a linked list in Java.

Read the explanation provided by ChatGPT to better understand the differences between these two data structures in Java.

Example 3: Input: "What should I do if I get a 'SyntaxError' in my JavaScript code?" Output: ChatGPT provides suggestions for identifying and resolving syntax errors.

Use the suggestions provided by ChatGPT to troubleshoot the syntax error in your code. This way, you can identify and correct errors more quickly and effectively.

III. GETTING STARTED WITH CHATGPT

Seeing how ChatGPT has countless uses, it's no surprise more people are benefitting from its services. If you want to get started as well, here are some ways to start using ChatGPT.

As an AI language model, Chat GPT is not a platform that requires sign-up or registration. Instead, it is a pre-trained model that can be accessed through various platforms and applications. In this section, we will cover the different ways you can access ChatGPT and provide some information on how to get started.

1. **OpenAI API:** OpenAI offers an API (Application Programming Interface) that allows developers to access the power of ChatGPT and other OpenAI language models. To use the OpenAI API, you will need to sign up for an API key and set up your development environment. OpenAI offers documentation and tutorials to help you get started.

OpenAI is an artificial intelligence research laboratory with leading AI researchers and engineers worldwide. The mission of OpenAI is to create safe, beneficial artificial intelligence that will enhance human capabilities and improve the world. In addition, OpenAI provides various tools and resources for developers, researchers, and businesses to build and utilize advanced AI technologies.

One of the most popular tools provided by OpenAI is the GPT (Generative Pre-trained Transformer) language model. GPT is a machine-learning model that can generate human-like text based on the input given to it. This technology can be used for a wide range of applications, including content creation, language translation, chatbots, and more.

Another important tool provided by OpenAI is the API (Application Programming Interface), which allows developers to integrate OpenAI's advanced AI technologies into their applications and services. With the API, developers can access and utilize the GPT language model and other advanced AI technologies without requiring extensive AI expertise or infrastructure.

OpenAI is also actively involved in AI research, focusing on creating safe and beneficial artificial intelligence. Their research includes developing new AI algorithms, exploring the ethical implications of AI, and investigating ways to ensure that AI benefits everyone in society.

Overall, OpenAI offers a range of tools and resources for developers. From the GPT language model to the API and cutting-edge AI research, OpenAI is helping to advance the field of artificial intelligence and make AI more accessible and beneficial for everyone.

2. **Hugging Face:** Hugging Face is an open-source platform offering pre-trained language models, including ChatGPT, for developers and researchers. To use Hugging Face, you can sign up for a free account and access their models through their API or open-source libraries.

3. **Third-Party Applications:** ChatGPT is integrated into many third-party applications, such as chatbots, language learning apps, and writing assistants. To use ChatGPT through these applications, you will need to sign up or create an account with the specific application.

4. **Online Demos:** Some websites offer online demos allowing you to interact with ChatGPT without sign-up or registration. These demos are typically for language learning or writing assistance and provide limited features.

To get started with ChatGPT, you will need to determine which platform or application you want to use. Depending on your level of experience with programming and development, some options may be more accessible than others. For example, suppose you are new to programming or development. In that case, we recommend starting with online demos or third-party applications, as they require little to no setup and can provide a user-friendly interface.

Once you choose a platform, you can experiment with Chat GPT's capabilities. For example, you can input sentences or phrases and receive feedback on pronunciation, grammar, and vocabulary for language learning. For content creation, you can input a topic or question and receive suggestions for writing or research. Finally, for businesses, you can input a problem or goal and receive insights and solutions.

It's important to note that while Chat GPT can provide valuable assistance, it is not a replacement for human intelligence and expertise. Therefore, the suggestions and insights provided by Chat GPT should be carefully evaluated and verified before implementing them into your work or business.

SIGN UP TO OPEN AI

To use ChatGPT through OpenAI, you will need to sign up for an API key and set up your development environment. Here are the steps to sign up and get started with OpenAI:

1. First, visit the OpenAI website: Go to the OpenAI website at https://openai.com/.

2. Sign up for an account: Click on the "Get API Key" button in the top right corner of the homepage. You will be prompted to enter your email address and create a password to sign up for an account.

3. Apply for access to the API: After signing up for an account, you will need to apply for access to the OpenAI API. Click on the "API" tab in the top navigation bar and follow the instructions to apply for access. OpenAI will review your application and notify you via email once your access has been approved.

4. Set up your development environment: Once approved for access to the OpenAI API, you will need to set up your development environment to start using ChatGPT. OpenAI provides documentation and tutorials to help you set up your environment, depending on your programming language and framework. Some popular options include Python and TensorFlow.

5. Use the API: After setting up your development environment, you can start using the OpenAI API to access ChatGPT and other OpenAI language models. OpenAI provides documentation on how to use the API, including sample code and examples.

It's important to note that using the OpenAI API may require some programming knowledge and experience. If you are new to programming, start with third-party applications or online demos that provide a user-friendly interface. However, if you are comfortable with programming and want to customize your use of ChatGPT, the OpenAI API fully can provide a powerful and flexible tool.

CHOOSE YOUR PLAN

If you are interested in using the OpenAI API, you will need to choose a plan that best fits your needs. OpenAI offers several plans, each with different levels of access and features. Here are the steps to choose your plan in OpenAI:

1. First, visit the OpenAI website: Go to the OpenAI website at https://openai.com/.

2. Choose a plan: Click on the "Pricing" tab in the top navigation bar. You will see a list of plans with different access levels and features. Choose the plan that best fits your needs.

3. Review the details: Once you have selected a plan, review the details and features included in the plan. Make sure the plan includes the API access and features you need for your project or application.

4. Sign up: After reviewing the details, click on the "Get started" button to sign up for the plan. You will be prompted to enter your email address and create a password to create an account.

5. Provide payment information: Once you have signed up for a plan, you will need to provide payment information to activate your account. OpenAI accepts major credit cards and PayPal.

6. Access the API: After providing payment information, you can start using the OpenAI API to access ChatGPT and other language models. OpenAI provides documentation and tutorials to help you get started with the API.

It's important to note that OpenAI's plans vary in price, starting at a few hundred dollars per month and increasing based on the level of access and features. So make sure to choose a plan that fits your budget and provides the necessary features for your project or application.

ACCESS THE PLATFORM

Once you have signed up for a plan and provided payment information, you can start accessing the OpenAI API. Here are the steps to access OpenAI:

1. Log in to your account: Go to the OpenAI website at https://openai.com/ and log in to your account using your email address and password.

2. Navigate to the API: Click on the "API" tab in the top navigation bar to access the API dashboard.

3. Generate an API key: In the API dashboard, click on the "Generate API Key" button to create a new API key. You can name the API key and select the permissions you want to grant, such as access to ChatGPT or other language models.

4. Use the API key: Once you have generated an API key, you can start using it to access the OpenAI API. The API key can be used in your development environment or third-party applications integrating with OpenAI.

5. Access documentation and tutorials: OpenAI provides extensive documentation and tutorials to help you get started with the API and use ChatGPT and other language models. You can access this documentation in the API dashboard or OpenAI website.

IV. PROMP INJENIRING TIPS FOR USING CHATGPT

Prompt engineering is the process of designing and optimizing prompts for AI language models, such as GPT-4. The quality and effectiveness of the prompts used to train these models can significantly impact their performance and ability to generate accurate and useful outputs.

In prompt engineering, the goal is to create prompts that effectively convey the model's desired inputs and outputs while minimizing ambiguity, noise, and other factors that could reduce the model's accuracy or effectiveness. This involves selecting appropriate input formats, defining the expected output format, and considering any constraints or limitations that might impact the model's performance.

Prompt engineering also involves ongoing optimization and refinement of prompts to improve the accuracy and effectiveness of the model over time. It involves adjusting the prompts' language, structure, or content based on feedback and performance metrics generated during the model training and testing process.

Overall, prompt engineering is critical to developing and training effective AI language models and requires careful consideration and expertise in natural language processing, machine learning, and related fields.

There are several advantages of prompt engineering, including:

1. **Improved model performance:** By carefully designing and optimizing prompts, the resulting language models can be more accurate, effective, and efficient. This is because the prompts provide clear and relevant input and output expectations, which can help the model better understand and interpret the data.

2. **Increased model flexibility:** Well-designed prompts can help language models adapt to new tasks and data sources more easily since they provide a structured framework for processing and generating outputs. This can help reduce the need for retraining models from scratch, saving time and resources.

3. **Enhanced model generalization:** Effective prompts can also help language models generalize better to new and diverse data by providing a consistent and well-defined framework for interpreting inputs and generating outputs. This can improve the model's ability to handle variations in language, context, and other factors that can affect accuracy and effectiveness.

4. **Better model interpretability:** By understanding how prompts are formulated and optimized, it can be easier to interpret and explain the decisions and outputs generated by language models. This can build trust and understanding with stakeholders and end-users and facilitate the wider adoption of AI technologies.

Training an AI language model like GPT-4 to specialize in prompt engineering is a complex process that requires expertise in natural language processing, machine learning, and related fields. However, here are some general steps and considerations that can help guide the training process:

- **Gather a diverse and relevant dataset:** The first step in training a language model is to collect a diverse and relevant dataset of texts related to prompt engineering. This could include research papers, blog posts, online discussions, and other sources of information.

- **Preprocess and clean the dataset:** Once you have a dataset, you'll need to preprocess and clean it to remove any irrelevant or redundant information, standardize formatting and syntax, and ensure consistency across the data.

- **Train the GPT-4 model:** After preprocessing the data, you can train the GPT-4 model using the dataset you've assembled. This typically involves fine-tuning the existing GPT-4 architecture on your specific task and data using techniques like transfer learning.

- **Evaluate model performance:** Once the model is trained, you'll need to evaluate its performance on a separate test dataset to measure its accuracy, precision, recall, and other relevant metrics. This can help identify areas where the model is underperforming or overfitting and guide further optimization.

- **Continuously refine and optimize the model:** Finally, as you gather more data and gain more insight into the model's performance, you can continuously refine and optimize the model to improve its accuracy, generalization, and effectiveness. This can involve adjusting hyperparameters, adding additional layers or nodes, or experimenting with different input or output formats.

While these steps provide a high-level overview of the training process, it's important to note that prompt engineering is a complex and ongoing field that requires ongoing learning and adaptation. As such, it's important to stay up-to-date with the latest research and best practices in this area and to continuously evaluate and refine your approach to maximize the effectiveness of the AI language model.

BE SPECIFIC

To be specific in prompt engineering, you need to clearly understand the task or problem you are trying to solve and the data and models you are working with. This involves defining the input and output formats, identifying any constraints or requirements, and optimizing the prompts' language and structure to maximize the model's accuracy and effectiveness.

Here are some examples of how you can use chatGPT for prompt engineering:

1. **Formulating prompts for sentiment analysis:** If you are working on sentiment analysis, you can use chatGPT to help you formulate effective prompts that accurately capture the sentiment of a given text. For example, you can prompt the model to identify the sentiment of a specific text, such as a product review, and provide a numerical score or label indicating whether the sentiment is positive, negative, or neutral.

2. **Optimizing prompts for language modeling:** If you are working on language modeling, use chatGPT to optimize your prompts for better model performance. For example, you can experiment with different input formats, such as adding additional context or modifying the structure of the input sequence, and evaluate how these changes impact the model's accuracy and effectiveness.

3. **Generating new prompts for data augmentation:** If you are working on data augmentation, you can use chatGPT to generate new prompts or variations of existing prompts that can help improve the diversity and quality of your training data. For example, you can prompt the model to generate new sentences or phrases similar to existing prompts but with slight variations in language or structure.

4. **Evaluating prompt quality:** If you are working on prompt evaluation, you can use chatGPT to analyze the quality of existing prompts and provide feedback on how to improve them for better model performance. For example, you can prompt the model to generate outputs based on existing prompts and evaluate the accuracy and relevance of these outputs to identify any areas where the prompts can be improved.

Here's an example of a prompt generated by chatGPT:

INPUT: I want you to become a prompt generator. First, I will tell you a story genre, and you will generate a prompt for a short story that a student should continue.

OUTPUT: Sure, I can generate a prompt based on a given story genre. Please tell me the story genre you have in mind, and I'll do my best to generate a suitable prompt.

INPUT: This is the story genre: Thriller

OUTPUT: Great, here's a prompt for a thriller short story:

Prompt: "As she walked home alone late at night, Emily noticed that she was being followed. She quickened her pace, but the footsteps behind her only grew louder. Just as she was about to break into a run, she felt a hand on her shoulder and a voice whispered in her ear, 'Don't scream, but I need your help...'"

In this prompt, the student is asked to continue the story from the point where Emily is approached by a stranger who needs her help. The student could explore the mystery of the stranger's identity, why they need Emily's help and the dangers and risks of getting involved in a stranger's problems.

The prompt provides a clear and specific scenario that is designed to generate tension and suspense and gives the student plenty of room to explore different plot twists and character motivations.

Here's a more specific example of a prompt generated by ChatGPT:

INPUT: I want you to become a prompt generator. First, I will give you a book title, and you give me a potential plot of the book. The plot should include the main characters as well as the settings. The story should also include good morals for children ages 10 to 12.

OUTPUT: Sure, I can try to generate a plot based on a given book title. Please provide the book title you have in mind, and I'll do my best to generate a suitable plot that includes main characters, settings, and good moral for children ages 10 to 12.

INPUT: Title: The Prince and the Forgotten Castle

OUTPUT: Great, here's a potential plot for "The Prince and the Forgotten Castle":

In a far-off kingdom, a young prince named Alexander discovers a forgotten castle hidden deep in the forest. The castle has been abandoned for years, and Alexander is intrigued by its mysterious past. As he explores the castle, he meets a wise old caretaker named William, who tells him the story of how the castle was once a place of great beauty and joy until a wicked sorcerer cursed it and caused all its inhabitants to forget their past.

Determined to break the curse and restore the castle to its former glory, Alexander sets out on a quest to find the sorcerer and asks him to lift the curse. Along the way, he meets a group of loyal companions, including a brave knight named Sir George and a kind-hearted girl named Emily. Together, they face many challenges and obstacles, including treacherous forests, dangerous beasts, and the sorcerer's minions.

As they journey closer to the sorcerer's lair, Alexander learns important lessons about courage, determination, and the importance of friendship. He realizes that true power comes from within and that even the greatest obstacles can be overcome when we work together and believe in ourselves. In the end, Alexander's quest is successful, and the curse is lifted from the castle. The people who once forgot their past can finally remember their history and reclaim their home.

The moral of the story is that with determination, perseverance, and the help of loyal friends, even the greatest challenges can be overcome. As a result, children can learn the value of friendship, determination, and the importance of preserving history and tradition.

EXPERIMENT WITH PROMPTS

Priming is a technique used in natural language processing and machine learning to improve the quality and relevance of text generation by providing context or hints to the model. For example, in the case of GPT (Generative Pre-trained Transformer) language models, priming is the process of providing an initial sequence of text or keywords to guide the generation of subsequent text.

Priming in GPT models works by providing a context or seed to the model, which allows it to generate text that is more consistent with the context. The context can be in the form of a few words, a sentence, or even a paragraph and can be used to specify the topic, genre, style, or mood of the text to be generated.

The basic idea behind GPT priming is to leverage the pre-trained knowledge and capabilities of the GPT model to generate relevant and coherent text with the given context. By providing a prompt or seed text, GPT models can be fine-tuned or conditioned to generate more specific text relevant to the context.

The process of GPT priming involves the following steps:

1. **Choosing the context:** The first step in GPT priming is to choose the context or seed text that will guide the generation of subsequent text. The context can be a few words, a sentence, or a paragraph and should be relevant to the topic or theme of the text to be generated.

2. **Encoding the context:** Once the context is chosen, it must be encoded into a format that the GPT model can process. This involves converting the text into numerical representations, such as token IDs or embeddings, that the GPT model can understand.

3. **Generating text:** After the context is encoded, it is fed into the GPT model as input, along with any additional parameters or constraints. The model then generates text consistent with the context, using its pre-trained knowledge and language generation capabilities.

4. **Evaluating the output:** Once the text is generated, it needs to be evaluated to ensure that it is coherent, relevant, and meets the desired criteria. This can be done using perplexity, coherence, readability, or human evaluation metrics.

5. **Fine-tuning the model:** If the output is unsatisfactory, the GPT model can be fine-tuned by adjusting the parameters, context, or training data. This involves retraining the model on additional data, modifying the architecture, or changing the hyperparameters.

GPT priming can be used for various applications, including creative writing, chatbots, recommendation systems, and content generation. For example, GPT priming can provide a starting point or prompt for generating stories, poems, or dialogues in creative writing. In chatbots, GPT priming can be used to provide a context or topic for the conversation, improving the relevance and coherence of the responses. Also, in recommendation systems, GPT priming can be used to generate personalized recommendations based on user preferences or previous interactions.

Some best practices for GPT priming include:

1. Use relevant and specific context: The context provided for GPT priming should be relevant to the topic or theme of the text to be generated and should be specific enough to guide the generation process effectively.

2. Vary the length and complexity of the context: Depending on the application and goals, the length and complexity of the context provided for GPT priming can vary widely. In general, shorter and simpler contexts are easier for the model to process but may result in less specific or diverse output.

3. Use high-quality and diverse training data: The quality and diversity of the training data used to pre-train the GPT model can significantly impact the quality and relevance of the generated text. Therefore, using

high-quality and diverse training data is essential to ensure that the GPT model can learn the nuances and complexities of natural language. This includes a wide range of sources such as books, articles, and other textual data from different domains and genres.

4. When selecting training data, it is important to ensure that it is diverse and representative of the language and topics the model intends to generate text for. This helps to prevent the model from developing biases or being limited in its ability to generate text for certain topics or domains.

5. Furthermore, ensuring that the data is of high quality and free from errors or inconsistencies is also crucial. This includes cleaning the data, removing duplicates, and ensuring that the data is properly formatted and structured.

6. In addition to the quality and diversity of the training data, other factors, such as the size of the data set and the training methodology used, can also impact the effectiveness of the priming process. Therefore, it is important to carefully consider these factors when training a GPT model for priming.

Experimenting with prompts in ChatGPT can be done through the following steps:

1. Access a platform or tool that allows you to generate prompts using ChatGPT, such as OpenAI's GPT-4 Playground or Hugging Face's Transformers library.

2. Define the type of prompt you want to generate, such as a creative writing prompt, a research question, or a conversational prompt.

3. Specify the length and complexity of the prompt, depending on your needs and goals. For example, you can generate a short prompt that requires only a few sentences of response or a longer prompt that requires a detailed essay or story.

4. Provide relevant context or keywords that the ChatGPT model can use to generate the prompt. This can include specific topics, themes, genres, or styles.

5. Experiment with different prompt variations and observe how the ChatGPT model responds. You can modify the length, complexity, and context of the prompt, as well as the degree of creativity, coherence, and relevance of the generated responses.

6. Evaluate the quality and usefulness of the generated prompts based on your criteria and goals. For example, you can use metrics such as readability, coherence, relevance, originality, or engagement to assess the effectiveness of the prompts.

7. Refine and iterate the prompt generation process based on the feedback and insights gained from the experiments. You can adjust the parameters, context, and goals of the prompt generation and the selection and evaluation of the generated prompts to optimize the outcomes.

Here are some pointers to remember when experimenting with prompts in ChatGPT:

1. **Start with a clear objective:** Define your goals and objectives before experimenting with prompts. This will help you select the right parameters, context, and criteria for generating and evaluating the prompts.

2. **Use relevant context and keywords:** Provide context and keywords relevant to your topic, theme, or genre. This will help the ChatGPT model generate coherent, relevant, and engaging prompts.

3. **Be specific and concise:** Use specific and concise language in your prompt. This will help the ChatGPT model focus on the key ideas and concepts you want to explore.

4. **Experiment with different lengths and complexities:** Try generating prompts of different lengths and complexities and evaluate their quality and usefulness based on your criteria and goals.

5. **Evaluate the generated prompts critically:** Use metrics such as readability, coherence, relevance, originality, or engagement to assess the effectiveness of the generated prompts. Be critical and objective in your evaluation, and refine your prompt generation process based on the feedback and insights gained.

6. **Iterate and refine the prompt generation process:** Refine and iterate the prompt generation process based on the feedback and insights gained from the experiments. Adjust the parameters, context, and goals of the prompt generation and the selection and evaluation of the generated prompts to optimize the outcomes.

REVIEW AND EDIT

Reviewing and editing prompts is an important step in the prompt engineering process. It helps ensure the generated text is relevant, coherent, and appropriate for the intended use case.

When reviewing prompts, it is important to consider factors such as the accuracy of the content, the tone and style of the language, and the relevance to the task or domain. This involves carefully reading through the prompt and checking for any errors or inconsistencies in the text.

Once any issues have been identified, the prompt can then be edited to improve its quality and relevance. This may involve rewording sentences, adding or removing information, or adjusting the tone or style of the language.

It is also important to consider the intended audience when editing prompts. For example, prompts intended for children may require simpler language and more visual cues to help them understand the task or prompt.

In addition, having multiple reviewers or editors to provide feedback and ensure that the prompt is accurate and relevant from different perspectives is helpful. This can help to identify any biases or assumptions that may have been overlooked.

Reviewing and editing prompts is a critical step in the prompt engineering process to ensure that the generated text is high-quality, relevant, and appropriate for the intended use case.

Several indicators can help you determine if your prompt is effective:

1. **Completion rate:** If the completion rate for your prompt is high, the prompt is likely effective. Completion rate refers to the percentage of users who successfully complete the task or activity outlined in the prompt. A high completion rate suggests the prompt was clear and specific enough for users to understand and follow.

2. **Quality of responses:** If the responses to the prompt are of high quality, it is likely that the prompt is effective. The quality of responses can be measured by criteria such as accuracy, relevance, creativity, and complexity. If the majority of responses meet these criteria, it suggests that the prompt effectively elicited high-quality output from users.

3. **User feedback:** User feedback can provide valuable insights into the effectiveness of the prompt. You can collect feedback through surveys, interviews, or focus groups. Users may provide feedback on factors such as clarity, relevance, interest, and difficulty. If users consistently provide positive feedback, the prompt is likely effective.

4. **Time to complete:** If users are able to complete the prompt within a reasonable amount of time, the prompt is likely effective. Time to complete refers to the time it takes users to complete the task or activity outlined in the prompt. Users may become frustrated or lose interest if the prompt takes too long to complete.

5. **Achievement of learning objectives:** If the prompt is intended for educational purposes, you can evaluate its effectiveness by measuring the achievement of learning objectives. Learning objectives refer to the specific skills or knowledge users are expected to acquire through the prompt. If users are able to achieve these objectives successfully, it suggests that the prompt was effective in facilitating learning.

By considering these indicators, you can evaluate the effectiveness of your prompt and make adjustments as necessary to improve its quality and relevance for users.

ADDENDUM TO THE CHAPTER: PROMPT STORE/ MARKETPLACE SELL/BUY PROMPTS

Another way that ChatGPT can help users earn is through selling prompts.

Yes, you can sell prompts online. There are various online marketplaces where you can sell your prompts, such as Teachers Pay Teachers, Udemy, and Skillshare. These platforms allow you to create and sell educational resources, including prompts, to a global audience. You can also sell prompts on your website, blog, or social media channels.

Another platform you can use is Prompt Base.

Promptbase is a web-based platform that provides a range of tools and resources for generating, testing, and refining prompts for machine learning applications, including natural language processing (NLP) and text generation. The platform includes a large database of pre-built prompts and templates, and tools for customizing and testing prompts to meet specific needs.

The core features of Promptbase include the following:

1. **Prompt library:** Promptbase includes a library of pre-built prompts for various use cases, including chatbots, language translation, sentiment

analysis, and more. Users can browse the library to find prompts that meet their needs and customize them as necessary.

2. **Prompt builder:** The platform also includes a prompt builder tool that allows users to create custom prompts for their specific use case. The builder provides a range of customization options, including prompts for collecting user input, generating text output, and more.

3. **Prompt testing:** Promptbase includes a testing feature that allows users to test their prompts in real-time to evaluate their effectiveness and make adjustments as necessary. The testing feature provides a range of metrics and insights, such as user engagement, response time, and accuracy.

4. **Data management:** The platform provides tools for managing and integrating data with machine learning models. Users can upload and manage datasets, train machine learning models, and access various analytics and reporting tools.

5. **Collaboration:** Promptbase also provides collaboration features that allow users to work together on prompts and share them with others. Users can collaborate on prompts, share feedback and insights, and work together to refine and improve prompts over time.

Promptbase can be used in a variety of applications, including:

1. **Chatbots:** Promptbase can be used to create and refine prompts for chatbots, including prompts for collecting user input and generating text output. The platform can be used to create chatbots for customer service, marketing, and other use cases.

2. **Sentiment analysis:** Promptbase can be used to create and refine prompts for sentiment analysis, including prompts for classifying text as positive, negative, or neutral. This can be used in social media monitoring, customer feedback analysis, and more applications.

3. **Language translation:** Promptbase can be used to create and refine prompts for language translation, including prompts for translating text from one language to another. This can be used in language learning, travel, and more applications.

4. **Text generation:** Promptbase can be used to create and refine prompts for generating text, including prompts for generating product descriptions, news articles, and more. This can be used in content marketing, journalism, and more applications.

Overall, Promptbase provides powerful tools and resources for generating, testing, and refining prompts for machine-learning applications. Whether you're a data scientist, developer, or business owner, Promptbase can help you create effective, engaging prompts that drive results.

When selling prompts online, it is important to ensure they are highly relevant to your target audience. This will help you establish a reputation as a reliable and trustworthy provider of educational resources. You may also want to consider offering potential customers free samples or trials of your prompts to help build interest and generate sales.

Additionally, ensuring you have the necessary permissions and licenses to sell your prompts online is important. For example, if your prompts are based on copyrighted material, you may need to obtain permission from the copyright holder or purchase a license to use the material. You should also be aware of any legal requirements related to selling educational materials in your jurisdiction.

There are several factors to consider when determining if a prompt is worth selling:

1. **Quality:** A high-quality prompt should be engaging, thought-provoking, and relevant to the target audience. It should also be well-written and free from grammatical errors or other issues that could detract from the user's experience.

2. **Originality:** Your prompt should be unique and not readily available elsewhere. If it is similar to other widely available prompts, it may be less appealing to potential buyers.

3. **Target audience:** Consider who your prompt is intended for and whether there is a demand for prompts in that area. If your prompt is too niche, it may not appeal to a broad enough audience to justify selling it.

4. **Market research:** Conduct research to determine if a market for prompts in your chosen niche exists. Look for online forums or groups related to the topic and see if there is interest in prompts.

5. **Competition:** Assess the competition and determine if your prompt offers something unique or fills a gap in the market. If many similar prompts are already available, it may be difficult to stand out and make sales.

6. **Feedback:** Gather feedback from potential customers to see if they find your prompt useful and engaging. Consider offering a free trial or sample to get feedback before investing time and resources into creating and selling the prompt.

Ultimately, the success of a prompt will depend on its quality, originality, and appeal to the target audience. Conducting thorough research and gathering feedback can help you decide whether a prompt is worth selling.

V. EXPERIENCE SKYROCKETING PRODUCTIVITY GROWTH WITH CHATGPT

ChatGPT, a large language model trained by OpenAI, based on the GPT-4 architecture, has revolutionized the field of natural language processing (NLP) and has the potential to significantly boost productivity. Here are some ways in which ChatGPT can skyrocket productivity:

1. **Text Generation:** ChatGPT can be used to generate a variety of text, including articles, essays, summaries, product descriptions, and more. It can help content creators, writers, and marketers produce high-quality content much faster than if they did it manually.

2. **Language Translation:** ChatGPT can translate text between languages, making it easier for businesses to communicate with customers and partners in different countries. It can save a lot of time and money compared to hiring professional translators or manually translating text.

3. **Customer Support:** ChatGPT can also be used to automate customer support by answering common questions and providing helpful information to customers. This capability can reduce the workload of customer support agents and help customers get the information they need quickly and efficiently.

4. **Personalized Recommendations:** ChatGPT can analyze user behavior and provide personalized products, services, and content recommendations. It can help businesses improve customer satisfaction and increase sales.

5. **Data Analysis:** ChatGPT has the ability to analyze large amounts of data, such as social media feeds, customer feedback, and market

research, which can help businesses make informed decisions and identify trends and patterns that may not be immediately apparent.

6. Writing **Assistance:** ChatGPT can also be used to assist writers with tasks such as proofreading, editing, and generating new ideas. As a result, it can save writers time and help them produce higher-quality work.

7. **Research Assistance:** ChatGPT can assist researchers by providing access to a vast amount of knowledge and information. This capability can help researchers identify patterns, analyze data, and make more informed decisions.

8. **Creative Writing:** ChatGPT can be used to generate new ideas for creative writing projects, such as novels, short stories, and screenplays, helping writers overcome writer's block and come up with new and interesting plotlines.

9. **Automated Content Creation:** ChatGPT can also be used to automatically generate content for websites, blogs, and social media accounts. It can save businesses a lot of time and help them maintain a consistent content schedule.

10. **Language Learning:** ChatGPT can be used to help people learn new languages by providing translations, grammar explanations, and vocabulary practice, which can be a valuable tool for people who don't have access to formal language classes.

Overall, ChatGPT has the potential to significantly boost productivity across a variety of industries and use cases. With its abilities, ChatGPT is quickly becoming an essential tool for businesses and individuals looking to stay ahead of the curve in the digital age.

Here are some of the top benefits ChatGPT gives its users:

TIME-SAVING BENEFITS

ChatGPT, being an AI language model, can provide various time-saving benefits to its users. Here are some ways ChatGPT can help you save time:

1. **Generating content:** With the help of ChatGPT, you can generate content for a wide range of purposes, such as writing articles, creating social media posts, and drafting emails.

2. **Automating customer support:** ChatGPT can be used to automate customer support by responding to frequently asked questions and assisting customers in real time.

Automating customer support with ChatGPT involves creating chatbots that mimic human conversation and provide seamless and efficient customer service. By automating certain tasks, businesses can save time and resources and provide customers with faster and more consistent support.

Here are some examples of how ChatGPT can automate customer support:

FAQs: One of the most common use cases for chatbots is to provide answers to frequently asked questions. For example, a chatbot for an e-commerce website could answer questions about shipping times, return policies, and product specifications.

Order tracking: Another common use case for chatbots is to provide real-time updates on the status of customer orders. By connecting the chatbot to the company's order tracking system, customers can receive up-to-date information on their orders without waiting on hold or navigating through a complex phone tree. For example, a chatbot for a food delivery service could provide updates on the status of a customer's order, including estimated delivery time and the delivery driver's name.

Troubleshooting: Chatbots can also be used to provide basic troubleshooting support for customers who are experiencing technical issues. By providing a series of diagnostic questions and pre-written answers, the chatbot can help customers identify the source of the problem and provide instructions for resolving it. For example, a chatbot for a software company could help customers troubleshoot common issues like password resets, software updates, and connectivity problems.

Sales support: Chatbots can also be used to provide basic sales support, such as answering questions about products and services, providing product recommendations, and assisting with the checkout process. By programming the chatbot to recognize common sales-related queries and provide tailored responses, businesses can increase the chances of converting website visitors into customers. For example, a chatbot for an electronics retailer could provide product recommendations based on a customer's browsing history or offer discount codes to encourage a purchase.

Appointment scheduling: Chatbots can also be used to schedule appointments and reservations. Customers can book appointments and receive confirmation emails without interacting with a human representative by connecting the chatbot to the company's scheduling system. For example, a chatbot for a hair salon could allow customers to book haircuts, color treatments, and other services and provide real-time availability information.

In each of these examples, ChatGPT provides a faster and more convenient customer experience while reducing the workload on the company's customer support team. By automating routine tasks and providing pre-written answers, chatbots can free up human representatives to focus on more complex or high-priority issues. Additionally, chatbots can provide 24/7 support, allowing customers to get the help they need at any time without waiting for business hours.

3. **Improving efficiency in research:** ChatGPT can assist in research by generating summaries of research papers and articles and even helping to generate new research ideas. This can save researchers a lot of time sifting through large amounts of data and finding relevant information.

Here are some ways that ChatGPT can be used to improve efficiency in research:

Automatic summarization: One of the most time-consuming parts of research is going through a large amount of text and summarizing it. ChatGPT can be trained to summarize text and generate concise summaries of articles or reports. This can save researchers time and make it easier to identify relevant information quickly.

Example: A researcher needs to go through dozens of articles related to a specific topic. Instead of reading each article in its entirety, they can input the articles into a ChatGPT model trained on summarization and quickly get a summary of each article.

Answering research queries: Researchers often have specific questions that need to be answered in order to move forward with their research. ChatGPT can be trained to answer research queries and provide relevant information.

For example, A researcher needs to know the traditions of a specific country. Instead of spending time searching for the answer, they can input the question into a ChatGPT model trained on answering questions and quickly get the answer they need.

Generating content: ChatGPT can be used to generate content such as research papers, reports, or even emails. This can save time and help researchers focus on other aspects of their research.

Example: A researcher needs to write a report on a specific topic. Instead of starting from scratch, they can input key points and research findings into a ChatGPT model trained on generating reports and quickly get a draft of the report. They can then edit and refine the content to meet their specific needs.

Data analysis: ChatGPT can be used to analyze large datasets and provide insights for research.

Example: A researcher has collected data on customer behavior and needs to identify patterns and trends. They can input the data into a ChatGPT model trained on data analysis and quickly get insights for their research.

Translation: ChatGPT can translate text from one language to another, making it easier for researchers to access information from sources in other languages.

Example: Instead of hiring a translator or spending time learning the language, researchers can input any text into a ChatGPT model trained on translation and quickly get a translated version of the text.

Using ChatGPT, researchers can save time, focus on other aspects of their research, and increase the accuracy and quality of their work.

4. **Enhancing writing skills:** ChatGPT can also improve writing skills by suggesting edits and rephrasing sentences. This can save time in the editing process and help writers produce better-quality content.

There are several ways in which ChatGPT can be used to enhance writing skills. Here are some examples:

Writing prompts: ChatGPT can generate writing prompts that can help writers overcome writer's block and come up with new ideas. These prompts can be customized based on the writer's preferences and cover various genres, styles, and topics.

Sentence completion: Another way to enhance writing skills is by using ChatGPT to complete sentences. This can help writers develop their sentence structure and syntax by seeing how the AI model would complete their sentences. It can also provide inspiration for new ideas and angles.

Summarization: ChatGPT can also be used for summarization, which is the process of condensing longer texts into shorter versions. This can be useful for writers who need to write a synopsis or a summary of a longer piece or for readers who want to get the gist of a longer text quickly.

Proofreading: ChatGPT can be used to proofread and edit text. While it may not replace human editors entirely, it can help catch basic grammatical errors, typos, and inconsistencies.

Writing coaching: ChatGPT can also be used for writing coaching, providing feedback on writing style, tone, and voice. This can be especially useful for beginner writers still developing their writing skills.

Overall, Chat GPT can be a valuable tool for writers looking to improve their writing skills.

5. **Streamlining workflows:** ChatGPT can be integrated into various workflows and processes to automate tasks and streamline workflows. For example, ChatGPT can generate meeting agendas, summarize meeting minutes, and even generate reports automatically.

Streamlining workflows is one of the key benefits of using ChatGPT. With the help of AI-powered automation and natural language processing, ChatGPT can significantly reduce manual tasks, improve accuracy, and increase productivity.

Here are some ways to streamline workflows using ChatGPT and some examples:

Automate repetitive tasks: ChatGPT can automate repetitive tasks such as data entry, scheduling, and report generation. For example, if you need to schedule a meeting, you can use a chatbot powered by ChatGPT to automate the scheduling process. The chatbot can access your calendar, find available slots, and send invitations to attendees.

Improve data analysis: ChatGPT can help streamline the data analysis process by automating data extraction, cleaning, and visualization. For example, if you need to analyze a large dataset, you can use ChatGPT to automate the data cleaning process, which can be time-consuming and error-prone if done manually.

Improve communication: ChatGPT can improve communication and collaboration among team members by providing a centralized platform for communication. For example, you can use ChatGPT to create a chatbot that can answer common questions, provide feedback, and inform team members of important updates.

Improve project management: ChatGPT can help streamline project management by automating task assignments, progress tracking, and deadline reminders. For example, you can use ChatGPT to create a chatbot that can assign tasks to team members, track progress, and send reminders when deadlines are approaching.

Improve documentation: ChatGPT can help streamline the documentation process by automating transcription, translation, and summarization tasks. For example, you can use ChatGPT to create a chatbot that can transcribe audio or video recordings, translate documents into different languages, and summarize long texts.

Improve recruiting: ChatGPT can help streamline the recruiting process by automating tasks such as resume screening, candidate outreach, and interview scheduling. For example, you can use ChatGPT to create a chatbot that can screen resumes for specific keywords, reach out to candidates via email or chat, and schedule interviews based on availability.

In conclusion, ChatGPT can be a powerful tool for streamlining workflows and improving efficiency in a variety of fields, which can help businesses and individuals save time and increase productivity.

6. **Personalized recommendations:** Personalizing recommendations using ChatGPT can be a powerful way to enhance the customer experience and drive sales. By leveraging the language model's natural language processing capabilities, businesses can generate personalized customer recommendations based on their preferences, past purchases, and other

data. This can save time in sifting through large amounts of information and help users find relevant information quickly.

Here are some steps and examples of how to personalize recommendations using ChatGPT:

Collect Customer Data: The first step to personalizing recommendations is to collect customer data. This can include their browsing history, purchase history, demographic information, and other relevant data.

Analyze the Data: Once you have collected customer data, you need to analyze it to identify patterns and trends. This can help you understand what products or services are most popular among certain segments of your customer base.

Train ChatGPT: After analyzing the data, you can train ChatGPT to generate personalized recommendations based on the customer's data. This can be done by inputting the customer's data into the model and using it to generate recommendations based on their past behavior and preferences.

Implement the Recommendations: Once the recommendations have been generated, you can display them on your website or in your app. This can be done through a recommendation engine that uses ChatGPT to generate personalized recommendations for each customer.

EXAMPLES

E-commerce: An e-commerce store can use ChatGPT to generate personalized customer recommendations based on purchase history and browsing behavior. For example, ChatGPT can recommend similar products, such as gluten-free or vegan options, if a customer frequently buys organic food products. This would enhance the customer experience and drive sales by providing relevant and personalized product recommendations.

Streaming Services: Streaming services like Netflix can use ChatGPT to generate personalized user recommendations based on their viewing history and preferences. For example, if a user frequently watches action movies, ChatGPT can recommend similar movies or TV shows that fit their interests. This can keep users engaged and increase their satisfaction with the service.

Banking and Financial Services: Banks and financial services providers can use ChatGPT to generate personalized customer recommendations based on their spending habits and financial goals. For example, if a customer frequently spends money on dining out, ChatGPT can recommend a credit card that offers rewards for dining purchases. This can help customers achieve their financial goals and increase their loyalty to the bank.

Travel: Travel companies can use ChatGPT to generate personalized customer recommendations based on their travel history and preferences. For example, if a customer frequently travels to beach destinations, ChatGPT can recommend similar destinations with similar activities or accommodations.

Personalizing recommendations using Chat GPT can be a powerful way to enhance the customer experience and drive sales.

7. **Speeding up language translation:** ChatGPT can be used to speed up the language translation process by generating machine translations that are more accurate and reliable than traditional translation software.

Language translation is a complex and time-consuming process, but advanced technologies like chatGPT can help streamline and speed up the process.

Here are some ways chatGPT can be used to speed up language translation:

Automated translation: ChatGPT can be used to create automated translation tools that can translate text from one language to another. The model can be trained on large datasets of bilingual text to improve the accuracy of the translations. This can help speed up the translation process for large volumes of text, such as website content or legal documents.

Real-time translation: ChatGPT can also be used to create real-time translation tools to translate speech or text. This can be useful for international conferences or meetings where participants speak different languages. In addition, the chatGPT model can be integrated into speech recognition software to transcribe and translate spoken words in real time automatically.

Multilingual chatbots: ChatGPT can be used to create multilingual chatbots that can communicate with customers in their preferred language. This can be useful for businesses that operate in multiple countries and need to provide customer support in different languages. In addition, the chatGPT model can be trained on customer service data in multiple languages to improve the accuracy of the chatbot's responses.

Machine-assisted translation: ChatGPT can also assist human translators by providing suggestions for translations. This can help speed up the translation process and improve the accuracy of translations.

EXAMPLES:

Google Translate: Google Translate is an example of an automated translation tool that uses machine learning, including chatGPT, to improve the accuracy of translations. The model is trained on large datasets of bilingual text to improve the accuracy of translations.

Skype Translator: Skype Translator is an example of a real-time translation tool that uses chatGPT to transcribe and translate spoken words in real time. The chatGPT model is integrated into the speech recognition software to improve the accuracy of translations.

IBM Watson Language Translator: IBM Watson Language Translator is an example of a machine-assisted translation tool that uses chatGPT to provide translation suggestions. The model is trained on large datasets of translated text to provide accurate suggestions for translations based on the context of the text.

Amazon Translate: Amazon Translate is an example of an automated translation tool that uses chatGPT to improve the accuracy of translations.

In addition, ChatGPT can be used to quickly translate customer inquiries and responses, allowing customer service representatives to respond in the customer's language without the need for a human translator. This can lead to faster response times and improved customer satisfaction.

Another potential use case for ChatGPT in language translation is in news reporting. Journalists often need to quickly translate news articles from one language to another in order to reach a wider audience. ChatGPT can be trained on a large corpus of news articles in different languages and can help news organizations reach a broader audience.

ChatGPT can also be used to speed up language translation in many other fields, such as E-commerce and education. For example, E-commerce platforms can use ChatGPT to translate product descriptions and customer reviews into multiple languages, allowing them to sell to customers worldwide. Marketing teams can translate advertising copy and social media posts for global campaigns. Educators can use ChatGPT to translate educational materials for students who speak different languages.

Overall, ChatGPT has the potential to significantly speed up language translation in a wide range of industries and applications.

8. **Automated content moderation:** ChatGPT can automate content moderation by flagging inappropriate content and providing suggestions for appropriate edits. This can save time and resources that would otherwise be spent on manual content moderation.

Automating content moderation using ChatGPT can be a powerful tool in ensuring that online platforms are safe and free from harmful content.

Here are some ways to automate content moderation using ChatGPT and examples of how it can be applied in different contexts:

DEVELOP A CUSTOM MODEL FOR SPECIFIC TYPES OF CONTENT:

One way to automate content moderation using ChatGPT is to develop a custom model for specific types of content. For example, a social media platform may want to automatically flag and remove posts that contain hate speech or graphic violence. By training a ChatGPT model on a dataset of similar content, the platform can quickly and accurately identify problematic posts and take action.

USE CHATGPT TO IDENTIFY PATTERNS IN LARGE DATASETS:

Another way to automate content moderation using ChatGPT is to use it to identify patterns in large datasets. This can be especially useful for identifying trends and potential issues that may not be immediately apparent to human moderators. For example, a news website could use ChatGPT to identify patterns in reader comments that suggest a particular article is generating controversy or attracting spam.

COMBINE CHATGPT WITH OTHER AUTOMATED TOOLS:

ChatGPT can also be combined with other automated tools to improve content moderation. For example, a platform could use ChatGPT to generate summaries of long user reviews or comments and then use a sentiment analysis tool to determine whether the overall sentiment is positive or negative. This can help to quickly identify problematic content that may be buried in lengthy reviews or comments.

USE CHATGPT TO GENERATE AUTOMATED RESPONSES TO COMMON ISSUES:

ChatGPT can also be used to generate automated responses to common issues or questions. This can reduce the workload for human moderators and ensure that users receive a timely response to their queries. For example, a customer service chatbot could use ChatGPT to generate responses to common questions about shipping times, returns policies, or product availability.

Use ChatGPT through sentiment analysis: Sentiment analysis is the process of using natural language processing and machine learning techniques to analyze the emotional tone of a piece of text. For example, ChatGPT can be trained to identify and flag potentially inappropriate content based on the sentiment analysis of user-generated content.

For instance, social media platforms such as Facebook and Twitter use sentiment analysis to detect and remove hate speech, bullying, and other forms of abusive content. ChatGPT can also be used to automate sentiment analysis for online forums, comment sections, and other forms of user-generated content.

Use ChatGPT to identify spam and phishing attempts: ChatGPT can be trained to recognize patterns and characteristics common in spam and phishing messages, such as suspicious URLs, excessive use of capital letters or exclamation marks, or misspelled words.

For example, email providers like Gmail and Yahoo use machine learning algorithms to detect and filter out spam and phishing emails from users' inboxes. ChatGPT can also be used to automate content moderation for messaging platforms, online marketplaces, and other forms of digital communication.

##Implementing ChatGPT-based moderation: Once you have a ChatGPT model that is trained and ready to use, you can begin implementing it for content moderation. Of course, the exact implementation will depend on the platform you are using and the specific requirements of your moderation process, but some common steps include the following:

##Integrating the ChatGPT model with your platform: This step involves using an API to connect the ChatGPT model to your platform or incorporating the model into the platform's code directly.

Defining the criteria for moderation: You will need to determine what types of content you want the ChatGPT model to flag for moderation. This could include specific keywords, phrases, or topics known to be problematic.

Setting thresholds: You must also set thresholds for when the ChatGPT model should flag content for moderation. For example, you may want the model to flag any content it deems 80% certain is problematic.

Testing and refining: Once the ChatGPT model is integrated with your platform, you can begin testing it to see how well it performs. You may need to refine the model and adjust the criteria and thresholds as you learn more about its performance.

Here are some examples of how ChatGPT-based moderation can be used:

Social media platforms: ChatGPT models can be used to automatically flag potentially problematic posts or comments on social media platforms, including hate speech, harassment, or other types of abusive content.

Online communities: ChatGPT models can be used to monitor online communities for rule violations, such as spam or off-topic posts.

E-commerce platforms: ChatGPT models can be used to flag potentially fraudulent or misleading product listings on e-commerce platforms.

Gaming platforms: ChatGPT models can be used to monitor the in-game chat and flag potentially inappropriate language or behavior.

By using ChatGPT-based moderation, platforms can save significant amounts of time and resources compared to manual moderation. In addition, ChatGPT models can often be more effective than human moderators at detecting problematic content, as they can process large amounts of data quickly and consistently. However, it is important to note that ChatGPT-based moderation is not a perfect solution and may still require human oversight to ensure that false positives are minimized, and legitimate content is not mistakenly flagged.

Overall, automating content moderation using ChatGPT can save time and resources for businesses, reduce the risk of reputational damage, and improve the user experience by creating a safer and more welcoming online environment.

9. **Customized chatbots:** ChatGPT can be used to create customized chatbots that can assist users in various tasks, such as booking appointments, answering FAQs, and even providing recommendations for products and services. This can save businesses time and resources that would otherwise be spent on manual customer support.

Customizing chatbots using ChatGPT involves using the model to create chatbots that can handle specific tasks or interact with users in a more personalized manner. Here are some steps to follow when customizing chatbots using ChatGPT:

Determine the chatbot's purpose and scope: Before beginning to customize a chatbot, it's important to determine its purpose and the scope of its capabilities. This will help identify the type of language models required and how the chatbot should respond to different user inputs.

Train the chatbot using relevant data: Once the scope and purpose of the chatbot have been determined, the next step is to train the chatbot using relevant data. This data could come from sources such as customer service interactions, social media conversations, or any other relevant sources.

Use pre-trained language models to improve chatbot capabilities: ChatGPT can be used to improve the chatbot's capabilities by providing pre-trained language models that can handle specific tasks. For example, a pre-trained language model specializing in customer service interactions can help the chatbot handle customer queries more effectively.

Use ChatGPT to generate more natural-sounding responses: ChatGPT can also be used to generate more natural-sounding responses tailored to the user's input. This can be achieved by training the model using a large dataset of natural language interactions.

Use ChatGPT to improve chatbot understanding of context: ChatGPT can help chatbots understand the context better by training the model using contextual information. This can help chatbots provide more relevant responses to users.

Here are some examples of how ChatGPT can be used to customize chatbots:

Personalized shopping assistance: Chatbots can be customized to provide personalized shopping assistance to users. For example, a chatbot can be trained using past purchases and browsing history data to suggest products relevant to the user's interests.

Improved customer service: Chatbots can be customized to provide improved customer service using pre-trained language models specializing in customer interactions. This can help chatbots provide more effective responses to customer queries.

Virtual assistants: Chatbots can be customized as virtual assistants that can help users with tasks such as scheduling appointments, setting reminders, and more.

Social media chatbots: Chatbots can be customized to interact with users on social media platforms. For example, a chatbot can be used to answer frequently asked questions, provide product recommendations, or assist with customer service issues.

Educational chatbots: Chatbots can be customized to provide educational content to users. For example, a chatbot can be trained to answer questions about a specific topic, provide explanations, and suggest additional resources.

Creating more natural and engaging conversations: Chatbots powered by GPT can be programmed to generate more natural and engaging conversations with users. This can be achieved by training the model on a large dataset of human interactions, allowing it to learn how to respond to users in a way similar to how a human would. Additionally, GPT can be used to generate more personalized responses based on the user's past interactions with the chatbot.

Example: A customer service chatbot for an e-commerce store can be customized using ChatGPT to provide more natural and engaging responses to customer queries. The chatbot can learn how to respond as a human customer service representative would by training the model on a large dataset of customer interactions. Additionally, ChatGPT can be used to generate more personalized responses based on the customer's purchase history and preferences.

Improving language understanding: ChatGPT can be used to improve language understanding in chatbots by training the model on a large dataset of text data, such as customer support tickets, emails, and social media messages. This allows the chatbot better to understand the context of the user's messages and provide more accurate and relevant responses.

Example: A travel chatbot can be trained using ChatGPT to understand the context of customer inquiries better. The chatbot can better understand the user's questions and provide more accurate and relevant responses by training the model on a large dataset of travel-related text data. For example, if a customer asks, "What are some good hotels in Paris?" the chatbot can use its understanding of the context to provide personalized recommendations based on the customer's budget and preferences.

Improving chatbot accuracy: ChatGPT can be used to improve the accuracy of chatbots by providing more training data to the model. By training the model on a larger dataset of text data, the chatbot can learn to understand the user's questions better and provide more accurate responses.

Example: A chatbot for a healthcare provider can be trained using ChatGPT to improve its accuracy in answering patient questions. The chatbot can learn to understand the context of patient inquiries and provide more accurate responses by training the model on a large dataset of healthcare-related text data. This can reduce the workload of healthcare providers by providing patients with accurate and timely information.

In conclusion, ChatGPT can be used to customize chatbots and improve their performance in various ways, including improving language understanding, accuracy, and personalization. Furthermore, by utilizing the power of machine learning and natural language processing, ChatGPT can help businesses provide more efficient and effective customer support, streamline workflows, and improve the overall user experience.

10. **Virtual assistants:** ChatGPT can be used to create virtual assistants that can assist users in various tasks, such as scheduling appointments, setting reminders, and even providing weather updates. This can save individuals time and make their daily lives more efficient.

ChatGPT can be a powerful tool as a virtual assistant, providing a wide range of capabilities to help streamline tasks and increase productivity. Here are some examples of how ChatGPT can be used as a virtual assistant:

Scheduling and Reminders: ChatGPT can be used to schedule meetings and appointments, set reminders, and even send notifications to remind you of upcoming events. For example, ask ChatGPT to schedule a meeting with a coworker at a specific time, and it will create the calendar event and send an invitation to the other party.

Email Management: ChatGPT can help manage your email by sorting through incoming messages, flagging urgent messages, and even drafting responses to common questions. You could ask ChatGPT to search your inbox for messages from a specific sender, and it will return a list of all the relevant messages.

Task Management: ChatGPT can help manage tasks by creating to-do lists, setting deadlines, and sending reminders. For example, you could ask ChatGPT to create a to-do list for a specific project and set deadlines for each task.

Information Retrieval: ChatGPT can help retrieve information quickly and easily. For example, you could ask ChatGPT to look up a definition, find a specific article, or even perform a quick calculation.

File Management: ChatGPT can help manage files by organizing them into folders, renaming them, and even creating backups. For example, you could ask ChatGPT to create a new folder and move all the relevant files.

Personal Assistant: ChatGPT can also serve as a personal assistant, providing recommendations for restaurants, hotels, and other services. For example, you could ask ChatGPT to recommend a good restaurant in a specific location, which will return a list of options.

Travel Planning: ChatGPT can assist with travel planning by finding flights, hotels, and rental cars. For example, you could ask ChatGPT to find the cheapest flight to a specific destination and provide you with a list of options.

Personalized News and Updates: ChatGPT can also provide personalized news and updates based on your interests. For example, you could ask ChatGPT to provide you with the latest news on a specific topic, which will return a list of relevant articles.

ChatGPT can be a powerful virtual assistant, helping streamline tasks and increase productivity. Its ability to quickly retrieve information, manage tasks, and provide personalized recommendations makes it an invaluable tool for both personal and professional use.

In summary, ChatGPT can save time and enhance productivity in various ways, from automating tasks to providing personalized recommendations and enhancing writing skills. Furthermore, as AI technology continues to advance, ChatGPT is likely to become even more powerful in the future, offering even greater benefits for users seeking to optimize their time and efficiency.

IMPROVED CONTENT QUALITY

ChatGPT can be used to improve content quality by generating high-quality content that can be used as a reference or inspiration for writers. Here are some ways to use ChatGPT to improve content quality:

1. **Generating topic ideas:** ChatGPT can be used to generate topic ideas for your content. Simply provide a general topic or keyword and let ChatGPT generate a list of related topics or angles to explore. This can help you come up with unique and interesting content ideas that you may not have thought of otherwise.

Generating topic ideas is one of the common use cases of ChatGPT.

Here are some ways to generate topic ideas using ChatGPT, along with examples:

1) **Seed phrases:** Start with a specific topic or keyword and use it as a seed phrase to generate related topics. For example:

Seed phrase: "Healthy Eating"

Generated topic ideas:

"The Benefits of Eating More Vegetables"

"Low-Calorie Snack Ideas for Weight Loss"

"Tips for Meal Planning on a Budget"

"Superfoods That Boost Your Immune System"

"Easy and Healthy Breakfast Ideas"

2) **Random sampling:** Use the random sampling feature of ChatGPT to generate a set of topic ideas based on a general category or theme. For example:

Theme: "Technology"

Generated topic ideas:

"The Future of Virtual Reality Technology"

"The Pros and Cons of Social Media for Businesses"

"The Ethics of AI in Healthcare"

"The Evolution of Mobile Technology"

"Cybersecurity: Tips for Staying Safe Online"

> 3) **Word association:** Use word association to generate a list of related topics. For example:

Word association: "Travel"

Generated topic ideas:

"The Best Budget Destinations for Solo Travelers"

"Eco-Friendly Travel Tips: How to Reduce Your Carbon Footprint"

"The Most Beautiful Beaches in the World"

"The Rise of Adventure Tourism"

"Exploring Different Cultures: The Benefits of Traveling Abroad"

> 4) **Trend analysis:** Use ChatGPT to analyze current trends and generate related topics. For example:

Trend: "Sustainability"

Generated topic ideas:

"Sustainable Fashion: Tips for Eco-Friendly Shopping"

"Green Living: How to Reduce Your Environmental Impact"

"The Future of Renewable Energy Sources"

"Sustainable Agriculture: Farming for the Future"

"The Impact of Climate Change on Our Oceans"

5) **Opposite approach:** Use the opposite approach to generate topics that challenge common beliefs or assumptions. For example:

Opposite approach: "Sleeping Less is Better"

Generated topic ideas:

"The Importance of Sleep for Overall Health"

"The Dangers of Sleep Deprivation"

"Tips for Better Sleep: How to Get More Restorative Sleep"

"The Science of Sleep: Why We Need 7-9 Hours of Sleep"

"Sleeping Better: The Benefits of Developing a Nighttime Routine"

ChatGPT can be a powerful tool for generating topic ideas for various content types, such as blog posts, articles, and videos.

2. **Generating outlines:** Once you have a topic, ChatGPT can help you generate an outline for your content. By providing a brief description of what you want to cover, ChatGPT can generate an outline that includes subtopics, key points, and a general structure for your content. This can save you time and help you stay organized as you write.

Generating an outline in ChatGPT is a useful way to organize your thoughts and ideas for writing.

Here are the steps to generate an outline using ChatGPT:

Start by identifying the main topic or idea for your writing piece. For example, if you're writing an article about the benefits of meditation, your main topic would be meditation.

Use ChatGPT to generate a list of subtopics related to your main topic. You can do this by providing a prompt like "What are some subtopics related to the benefits of meditation?" ChatGPT will generate a list of subtopics based on its understanding of the topic.

Review the list of subtopics generated by ChatGPT and select the ones that are most relevant to your writing piece. For example, some of the subtopics generated by ChatGPT might include "improved focus," "stress reduction," and "better sleep."

Use ChatGPT to generate a summary or description for each subtopic you've selected. This will help you further refine your outline and ensure you cover all the important points in your writing piece. For example, you could provide a prompt like "Can you briefly summarize the benefits of improved focus?" ChatGPT will generate a summary based on its understanding of the topic.

Use the subtopics and summaries generated by ChatGPT to create an outline for your writing piece. Start with the main topic and then list the subtopics underneath it. Finally, use the summaries to provide more detail about each subtopic.

Here's an example of an outline for an article about the benefits of meditation:

I. Introduction

A. Definition of meditation

B. Brief history of meditation

II. Benefits of meditation

A. Improved focus

1. Increased productivity

2. Better decision making

B. Stress reduction

1. Lower cortisol levels

2. Reduced anxiety

C. Better sleep

1. Increased melatonin

2. Improved sleep quality

III. How to get started with meditation

A. Setting up a meditation practice

1. Choosing a quiet space

2. Setting a regular time

B. Types of meditation

1. Mindfulness meditation

2. Transcendental meditation

IV. Conclusion

A. Recap of benefits

B. Encouragement to try meditation

3. **Generating introductions:** The introduction is often the most important part of a piece of content, as it sets the tone for the rest of the piece. ChatGPT can be used to generate introductions that are engaging, informative, and relevant to your topic. The generated introductions can help grab your reader's attention and keep them engaged throughout the rest of the piece.

Generating introductions with ChatGPT can be a helpful tool for writers who struggle with writer's block or need inspiration for a new piece of content.

Here are some ways to generate introductions with ChatGPT, along with examples:

a) **Ask a Question:** One way to grab the reader's attention is to ask a question in the introduction. The question can be rhetorical or specific, depending on the topic. ChatGPT can be used to generate questions that are relevant to the topic and can help stimulate creativity. For example:

Topic: The Benefits of Exercise

Prompt: Generate an introduction for an article about the benefits of exercise.

Generated Introduction: Have you ever wondered why some people are so dedicated to exercising? What drives them to spend hours running on a treadmill or lifting weights? The answer is simple: the benefits of exercise are numerous and far-reaching.

b) **Use a Shocking Statistic:** Using a statistic in the introduction can be an effective way to grab the reader's attention and make them interested in the topic. ChatGPT can be used to generate relevant statistics that can be used to create a compelling introduction. For example:

Topic: The Effects of Climate Change on Sea Levels

Prompt: Generate an introduction for an article about the effects of climate change on sea levels.

Generated Introduction: Did you know that sea levels have risen by more than 8 inches since 1880? This increase is largely due to the effects of climate change, which is causing glaciers and ice caps to melt at an alarming rate.

c) **Tell a Story:** Starting with a story can effectively engage readers and draw them into the topic. ChatGPT can generate story ideas relevant to the topic, which can be used to create an engaging introduction. For example:

Topic: Overcoming Adversity

Prompt: Generate an introduction for an article about overcoming adversity

Generated Introduction: When Lisa was diagnosed with cancer, she thought her life was over. But through determination and a positive attitude, she was able to overcome the challenges she faced and emerge stronger than ever. Her story is a powerful reminder of the human capacity to overcome adversity.

    d) **Use an Analogy:** Analogies can creatively introduce a topic and help the reader understand complex ideas. ChatGPT can be used to generate analogies that are relevant to the topic, which can be used to create a memorable introduction.

For example:

Topic: Writing a Novel

Prompt: Generate an introduction for an article about writing a novel

Generated Introduction: Writing a novel is like embarking on a long journey. There will be ups and downs, twists and turns, but in the end, you will arrive at your destination proud of what you have accomplished. But how do you start? And how do you keep going when the going gets tough?

4. **Generating headlines:** A great headline can make or break your content. ChatGPT can help generate headlines that are attention-grabbing, relevant, and optimized for SEO. By briefly describing your content, ChatGPT can generate a list of potential headlines for you to choose from.

Generating headlines with ChatGPT can be useful for content creators and marketers looking to improve their content marketing strategy.

Here are some steps and examples of how to generate headlines using ChatGPT:

    a) **Define your topic:** Before generating a headline, you need to define the topic of your content. This will help ChatGPT understand the context and generate relevant and effective headlines.

89

b) **Choose the length and tone of your headline:** Depending on your audience and your content's purpose, you can choose a longer or shorter headline and a serious or playful tone.

c) **Input your topic into ChatGPT:** Once you have defined your topic and chosen the length and tone of your headline, you can input your topic into ChatGPT and let it generate headlines for you.

d) **Review and edit the generated headlines:** After ChatGPT generates a list of headlines for you, you should review and edit them to ensure they are relevant, catchy, and effective for your content.

Here are some examples of how to generate headlines using ChatGPT:

Topic: "10 Tips for Running a Successful Online Business"

Headline 1: "Expert Advice: 10 Tips to Make Your Online Business a Success"

Headline 2: "Maximize Your Online Business's Potential with These 10 Proven Tips"

Headline 3: "Ready to Build a Successful Online Business? Follow These 10 Tips"

Topic: "The Benefits of Meditation for Mental Health"

Headline 1: "Unlock the Power of Meditation: How It Can Improve Your Mental Health"

Headline 2: "Discover the Mental Health Benefits of Meditation: A Comprehensive Guide"

Headline 3: "Meditation: The Natural Way to Boost Your Mental Health and Well-being"

Topic: "The Future of Artificial Intelligence in Healthcare"

Headline 1: "The AI Revolution in Healthcare: What the Future Holds"

Headline 2: "The Game-Changing Potential of AI in Healthcare: A Closer Look"

Headline 3: "The Future of Healthcare: How AI is Changing the Landscape"

5. **Generating conclusions:** Like the introduction, the conclusion is important to your content. It should summarize your main points and give your reader a strong takeaway. ChatGPT can be used to generate clear, concise, and impactful conclusions.

Generating effective and impactful conclusions is an important part of any writing task, whether an essay, article, or research paper. Conclusions help to summarize the key points and findings of the writing and leave a lasting impression on the reader.

Here are some tips on how to use ChatGPT to generate conclusions and some examples:

a) **Input the main ideas:** To generate a conclusion, it is important to input the main ideas and findings of the writing. This will allow ChatGPT to generate a conclusion that accurately summarizes the key points of the writing.

b) **Be clear and concise:** Conclusions should be clear and concise to effectively summarize the writing. Ensure that the language used is straightforward and easy to understand.

c) **Use impactful language:** To leave a lasting impression on the reader, use impactful language. This can be achieved by using strong verbs and adjectives.

Here are some examples of how ChatGPT can be used to generate conclusions:

Topic: The Benefits of Meditation

Input: "Meditation has numerous benefits, including reducing stress and anxiety, improving focus and attention, and promoting emotional well-being."

Output: "In conclusion, meditation is a powerful tool that can help reduce stress and anxiety, improve focus and attention, and promote emotional well-being. With its many benefits, it is worth considering making meditation a regular part of your daily routine."

Topic: The Effects of Climate Change on Biodiversity

Input: "Climate change has had a significant impact on biodiversity, causing changes in ecosystems and threatening the survival of many species."

Output: "In summary, the effects of climate change on biodiversity are far-reaching and have the potential to cause significant harm to our planet's ecosystems. We must take action to reduce our carbon footprint and protect our planet's biodiversity before it is too late."

Topic: The Importance of Time Management for Students

Input: "Effective time management is essential for students to succeed academically, balance extracurricular activities, and maintain a healthy work-life balance."

Output: "In conclusion, time management is a critical skill for students to develop to succeed academically, balance extracurricular activities, and maintain a healthy work-life balance. By effectively managing their time, students can reduce stress and achieve their goals."

6. **Generating descriptions:** If you're creating content for products or services, ChatGPT can be used to generate product or service descriptions that are engaging, informative, and persuasive. By providing basic information about the product or service, ChatGPT can generate a description that highlights its key features and benefits.

Generating descriptions using ChatGPT can be a powerful tool for various tasks, such as writing product descriptions, travel descriptions, or even describing people, places, and things.

Here are some steps and examples of how to generate descriptions using ChatGPT:

a) **Identify the topic or object you want to describe:** The first step is to identify the object or topic you want to describe clearly. It could be a product, place, person, or anything that requires a detailed description.

b) **Provide some basic information:** To help ChatGPT generate a relevant and accurate description, provide some basic information about the object or topic. This could include its name, its purpose, its location, its features, or anything else that is important to know.

c) **Ask ChatGPT to generate a description:** Once you have provided the necessary information, ask ChatGPT to generate a description. Again, be specific about what you want to be described and provide any relevant details or parameters.

d) **Edit and refine the generated description:** While ChatGPT can produce a description, it may not always be perfect. Review the generated description and edit it as necessary to ensure accuracy and clarity. You can also refine the description to make it more compelling or interesting.

Example 1: Writing a Product Description

Let's say you are tasked with writing a description for a new coffee maker. Here is an example of generating a description using ChatGPT:

Input: Can you describe the new coffee maker we just launched?

Output: The new coffee maker is a sleek and modern appliance designed to make brewing coffee at home quick and easy. With its programmable features and intuitive controls, this coffee maker can be customized to suit your personal preferences and brewing needs. In addition, the coffee maker features a durable and long-lasting construction, and its compact size makes it ideal for use in small kitchens or offices. Whether you prefer strong, bold coffee or a milder blend, this coffee maker is sure to impress.

In this example, ChatGPT has generated a description highlighting the coffee maker's key features, including its programmable features, intuitive controls, and compact size. The description also mentions the coffee maker's durability and ability to brew a variety of coffee blends.

Example 2: Writing a Travel Description

Let's say you are writing a travel guide for a new destination. Here is an example of how to use ChatGPT to generate a description:

Input: Can you describe the city of Tokyo?

Output: Tokyo is a vibrant and bustling city famous for its cutting-edge technology, delicious food, and unique cultural experiences. From Shinjuku's towering skyscrapers to Asakusa's historic temples and shrines, Tokyo has something to offer everyone. In addition, the city is home to various world-class museums, galleries, and theaters, as well as some of the best shopping and dining in the world. So whether you are interested in history, art, or simply soaking up the sights and sounds of a new city, Tokyo is the perfect destination.

In this example, ChatGPT has generated a description highlighting Tokyo's key attractions and features, including its technology, food, and culture. The description also emphasizes the diversity of experiences available in the city, from museums and galleries to shopping and dining.

Example 3: Describing a Person

Let's say you need to describe a historical figure for a school project. Here is an example of how to use ChatGPT to generate a description:

Input: Can you describe Albert Einstein?

Output: Albert Einstein was one of the most influential scientists of the 20th century. He is best known for his groundbreaking work on the theory of relativity, which revolutionized our understanding of space and time. Einstein was also a passionate pacifist and civil rights advocate and was awarded the Nobel Prize in Physics in 1921 for his work on theoretical physics. He was born in Germany in 1879 and moved to the United States in 1933 to escape Nazi persecution. Einstein was known for his unconventional appearance, often seen with messy hair and wearing mismatched socks. Despite his fame, he remained humble and dedicated to his work until his death in 1955.

Using ChatGPT to generate a description can save time and provide a solid foundation for further research. Adding specific details or insights can also provide a starting point for crafting a more unique and personalized description.

Using ChatGPT to improve content quality saves you time, helps you stay organized, and generates engaging, informative, and optimized content for your target audience.

ENHANCED CREATIVITY

Creativity is crucial in many industries, including art, marketing, advertising, and innovation. Creativity enables individuals to think outside the box, develop unique solutions to problems, and develop new ideas. However, many people need help generating new ideas or creating creative solutions to problems. This is where ChatGPT comes in. In this part, we will explore how ChatGPT can enhance creativity.

Ways to Enhance Creativity using Chat GPT

1. Idea Generation

ChatGPT can be used to generate ideas by analyzing your input and using its knowledge of language to suggest new concepts or solutions.

For example, let's say you are working on a new marketing campaign for a product. You can input basic information about the product, such as its features and target audience, into ChatGPT, and it will generate new ideas for marketing slogans or ad copy. The generated ideas can then be used as a starting point for further brainstorming and refinement.

2. Content Creation

Another way that ChatGPT can enhance creativity is by generating content. Whether you are a writer, marketer, or content creator, generating fresh, relevant content is a constant challenge. ChatGPT can generate content by analyzing existing content and using its language knowledge to create new content that is relevant and engaging.

For example, if you are a blogger looking to generate new content ideas. You can input basic information about your blog's niche, such as the subject matter or target audience, into ChatGPT, which will generate new ideas for blog posts.

ChatGPT can enhance the idea-generation process by providing suggestions and inspiration based on the input it receives.

Here are some examples of how to generate ideas through Chat GPT:

A. Writing Prompt Ideas:

Input: Can you give me some prompt writing ideas for a fantasy story?

Output: 1) Write a story about a kingdom ruled by a young queen who must fight against dark magic to save her people.

2) Create a story about a young orphan who discovers he has magical powers and journeys to find his true identity.

3) Write a story about a group of unlikely heroes who unite to defeat a powerful evil threatening their world.

B. Marketing Campaign Ideas:

Input: Can you give me some marketing campaign ideas for a new product launch?

Output: 1) Create a social media campaign encouraging users to share photos of themselves using the product with a branded hashtag.

2) Launch a referral program that rewards customers who refer friends to purchase the product.

3) Develop a targeted email campaign highlighting the product's unique features and benefits.

C. Blog Post Ideas:

Input: Can you give me some blog post ideas for a personal finance blog?

Output: 1) Write a post about the best investment strategies for beginners.

2) Create a post about the top money-saving apps to use in 2021.

3) Write a post about the benefits and drawbacks of using credit cards.

D. Video Content Ideas:

Input: Can you provide video content ideas for a cooking channel?

Output: 1) Create a series of instructional videos on how to make the perfect pizza.

2) Launch a "Cooking with Kids" series with easy-to-follow recipes for parents and children to make together.

3) Produce a "Cooking Around the World" series that explores the unique cuisine of different cultures.

E. Product Development Ideas:

97

Input: Can you provide some product development ideas for a fitness brand?

Output: 1) Develop a smartwatch app that provides personalized workout plans based on user fitness levels and goals.

2) Launch a line of eco-friendly workout gear made from recycled materials.

3) Create a fitness tracking device that can be used to monitor and track progress during workouts.

By inputting different prompts and questions into ChatGPT, users can receive a wide range of ideas and suggestions, ultimately improving the quality of their work.

3. Improving Writing Skills

ChatGPT can also be used to improve writing skills by providing suggestions for improving grammar, sentence structure, and word choice. This can be especially useful for non-native speakers or those who need help with writing. By inputting a text into ChatGPT, it can provide suggestions for improving the text, such as suggesting alternative words or sentence structures.

4. Enhancing Design

ChatGPT can also be used to enhance design by generating new design concepts or suggesting improvements to existing designs. This can be especially useful for graphic designers or those working on creative projects.

For example, you are a graphic designer working on a new logo design for a client. You can input some basic information about the client and their brand into ChatGPT, and it will generate new logo concepts or suggest improvements to existing designs.

ChatGPT can also enhance designs by providing suggestions and inspiration for design elements, such as color schemes, typography, and layout. Here are some examples of how to use ChatGPT to enhance designs:

Color Schemes

Input: Can you suggest a color scheme for a handmade crafts website?

Output: For a website selling handmade crafts, I suggest using warm colors, such as shades of orange and red, which evoke creativity and passion. You could also incorporate earthy tones like browns and greens to create a natural and rustic feel.

Typography

Input: Can you suggest a font for a logo for a new startup company?

Output: For a startup company, I suggest using a bold and modern font like Futura or Montserrat. These fonts convey a sense of innovation and forward-thinking, which is important for a new company looking to establish itself in a competitive market.

Layout

Input: Can you suggest a layout for a brochure for a travel agency?

Output: For a travel agency brochure, I would suggest using a clean and simple layout with plenty of white space to showcase the beautiful destinations. You could use a two or three-column layout with high-quality images and short, descriptive paragraphs to highlight the unique features of each location.

Overall Design

Input: Can you provide some design inspiration for a restaurant menu?

Output: For a restaurant menu, I suggest using a modern and sophisticated design with clean lines and bold typography. You could use a muted color palette with accents of bright colors to draw attention to certain items on the menu. Incorporating high-quality images of the dishes can also make the menu more visually appealing.

Using ChatGPT to enhance designs, designers can save time and gain inspiration and guidance on design elements they may not have considered otherwise. It can also help ensure consistency in design across different projects and clients.

5. Improving Collaboration

ChatGPT can also improve collaboration between team members by providing a platform for sharing and refining ideas. By inputting ideas into ChatGPT, team members can receive suggestions for improvement and refine their ideas until they are fully developed. ChatGPT can also facilitate communication between team members, allowing them to quickly and easily share ideas and feedback.

For example, imagine a marketing team tasked with developing a new advertising campaign for a product. They could use ChatGPT to generate a list of potential slogans, taglines, and themes based on the product's key features and target audience.

6. Enhancing Learning and Education

ChatGPT can also be a valuable tool for enhancing learning and education. Students and educators can use ChatGPT to generate topic ideas, research questions, and outlines for papers and projects. They can also use ChatGPT to generate summaries and synopses of academic articles and books, making it easier to digest and understand complex information.

For example, a student tasked with writing a research paper on the history of the Civil Rights Movement could input a prompt into ChatGPT asking for a list of key events and figures to include in their paper. ChatGPT could generate a list of relevant topics and subtopics, which the student could then use as the basis for their research and writing.

Another example is an educator using ChatGPT to create lesson plans and course materials. They could input a prompt asking for ideas on how to teach a particular concept or topic, and ChatGPT could generate a variety of activities, discussion questions, and multimedia resources to engage students and enhance their understanding.

ChatGPT is a powerful tool for enhancing creativity, productivity, and efficiency in various fields. By leveraging the power of artificial intelligence and natural language processing, ChatGPT can generate ideas, streamline workflows, and facilitate communication and collaboration between individuals and teams.

VI. CHATGPT TO CREATE PASSIVE INCOME STREAMS

In today's fast-paced world, everyone is looking for ways to earn extra income. Passive income is a popular choice for people who want to earn money without actively working. There are many ways to create passive income streams, such as investing in stocks, renting properties, or starting an online business. However, one lesser-known way to create passive income streams is by using ChatGPT.

This section will explore how you can use ChatGPT to create passive income streams.

AFFILIATE MARKETING

Affiliate marketing is performance-based marketing where an affiliate promotes a product or service and earns a commission for every sale or referral made through their unique affiliate link. In recent years, chatbots have become an increasingly popular tool for affiliate marketers to promote products and services to their audience. Chatbots can be integrated into social media platforms, websites, and messaging apps, allowing affiliate marketers to reach their audience in a more personalized and engaging way.

How to use ChatGPT to enhance affiliate marketing strategies?

1. **Use ChatGPT to create engaging content:**

One of the most effective ways to promote affiliate products and services is by creating engaging and informative content highlighting their benefits and features. ChatGPT can generate creative content ideas, write compelling product descriptions, and even develop entire articles or blog posts. By inputting a topic or keyword related to the product or service you are promoting, ChatGPT can provide you with various unique and interesting content ideas that will appeal to your target audience.

2. Personalize the affiliate marketing experience with ChatGPT:

Chatbots powered by ChatGPT can also create a more personalized affiliate marketing experience for your audience. For example, integrating a chatbot into your website or messaging app lets you engage with your audience in real time and provide them with personalized product recommendations, promotions, and offers based on their preferences and needs.

For example, if you are promoting a beauty product, you could create a chatbot that asks your audience about their skin type, concerns, and preferences and then provides them with personalized product recommendations based on their answers.

3. Use ChatGPT to automate social media marketing:

Social media platforms like Facebook, Instagram, and Twitter are great places to promote affiliate products and services. However, managing multiple social media accounts and creating engaging content can be time-consuming and challenging. ChatGPT can automate social media marketing tasks like scheduling posts, responding to comments and messages, and creating engaging content that resonates with your audience.

For example, you could use ChatGPT to schedule social media posts promoting a particular product or service, along with accompanying images and hashtags. You could also create a chatbot that responds to comments and messages on your social media accounts, providing your audience with personalized product recommendations and answering their questions about the products and services you are promoting.

4. Use ChatGPT to optimize your affiliate marketing campaigns:

Finally, ChatGPT can be used to optimize your affiliate marketing campaigns by providing valuable insights into your audience's preferences, interests, and behaviors. By analyzing data from your chatbot interactions, you can identify which products and services are most popular with your audience, which promotions and offers are most effective, and which marketing channels drive the most traffic to your affiliate links.

For example, you could use ChatGPT to track the number of clicks, conversions, and sales generated by your affiliate links, as well as your audience's geographic location and demographic information. By analyzing this data, you can determine which strategies and tactics are most effective in generating income and adjust your approach accordingly.

Another way to use ChatGPT in affiliate marketing is to generate content ideas and product recommendations for your audience. By inputting keywords related to your niche or the products you are promoting, ChatGPT can suggest topics and products you can feature on your website or social media channels. This can help you stay on top of industry trends and provide valuable content to your audience, leading to increased clicks and conversions.

BLOGGING AND CONTENT CREATION

Blogging and content creation are popular ways to generate passive income, and ChatGPT can be a valuable tool for improving the efficiency and quality of these processes. Here are some ways that ChatGPT can be used to enhance blogging and content creation as a means of generating passive income:

1. **Generating topic ideas:** One of the most challenging aspects of blogging and content creation is coming up with fresh and engaging topic ideas. ChatGPT can be used to generate topic ideas based on keywords or phrases. For example, if you are a food blogger, you could input "healthy recipes" into ChatGPT and receive a list of potential topics such as "10 easy meal prep recipes for a healthy week" or "5 healthy smoothie bowl recipes to start your day off right."

2. **Creating outlines:** Once you have a topic idea, ChatGPT can be used to create an outline for your post or article. By inputting the topic idea into ChatGPT, you can receive a list of subtopics and key points to include in your content. This can save time and ensure that your content is well-organized and informative.

3. **Writing introductions and conclusions:** ChatGPT can also be used to generate introductions and conclusions for your blog posts or articles. By inputting a brief summary of the topic and the key points you want to cover, ChatGPT can generate a compelling introduction and conclusion that engages readers and ties together the main ideas of your content.

4. **Enhancing content quality:** ChatGPT can be used to enhance the quality of your content by suggesting relevant statistics, examples, and quotes to support your arguments. By inputting a topic or keyword, ChatGPT can generate a list of relevant information that can be used to enrich your content and make it more engaging for your audience.

EXAMPLES:

1. **Fitness blogger:** A fitness blogger could use ChatGPT to generate topic ideas for their blog posts such as "10 ways to boost your metabolism" or "5 ways to stay motivated on your fitness journey." They could also use ChatGPT to create post outlines and suggest relevant statistics and studies which support their arguments.

2. **Personal finance blogger:** A personal finance blogger could use ChatGPT to generate topic ideas for their blog posts, such as "5 ways to save money on groceries" or "How to create a budget that works for you." They could also use ChatGPT to suggest relevant quotes and examples to support their arguments and make their content more engaging for their audience.

3. **Travel blogger:** A travel blogger could use ChatGPT to generate topic ideas for their blog posts, such as "10 must-see destinations in Europe" or "5 tips for traveling on a budget." They could also use ChatGPT to create outlines for their posts and suggest relevant statistics and facts about the destinations they are writing about.

In conclusion, ChatGPT can be a valuable tool for bloggers and content creators looking to generate passive income. By using ChatGPT to generate topic ideas, create outlines, and suggest relevant information, bloggers can save time and improve the quality of their content.

SOCIAL MEDIA MANAGEMENT

Social media management is a popular way to make money online, and ChatGPT can be a useful tool to automate and enhance your social media activities. Here are some examples of how you can use ChatGPT to generate passive income through social media management:

1. **Social Media Post Scheduling -** ChatGPT can automate the scheduling process of social media posts. By inputting your content ideas and keywords into ChatGPT, you can generate a list of potential social media posts. You can then use a social media scheduling tool, such as Hootsuite or Buffer, to schedule these posts to go out at optimal times throughout the day. This saves you time and ensures your social media profiles are consistently active.

ChatGPT makes it easier to manage multiple accounts and create a consistent posting schedule.

Here are some ways to use ChatGPT for scheduling social media posts:

a) **Create a content calendar:** Use ChatGPT to create a content calendar for your social media accounts. This can help you plan your posts in advance and ensure that you are consistently posting high-quality content.

Example input: "Can you create a content calendar for my Instagram account?"

Example output: "Here is a content calendar for your Instagram account: Monday: motivational quote, Tuesday: healthy recipe, Wednesday: before-and-after transformation story, Thursday: workout routine, Friday: progress update from a client, Saturday: a behind-the-scenes look at your fitness routine, Sunday: rest day inspiration."

b) **Schedule posts:** Use ChatGPT to schedule your social media posts in advance. This can save time and ensure that your posts are published at the optimal times for your audience.

Example input: "Can you help me schedule my social media posts for the week?"

Example output: "Sure, I can help you schedule your social media posts. Here are the best times to post for each platform: Monday: Instagram at 9 am, Tuesday: Twitter at 2 pm, Wednesday: Facebook at 1 pm, Thursday: LinkedIn at 10 am, Friday: Pinterest at 3 pm. I will schedule your posts accordingly."

2. **Social Media Content Creation -** ChatGPT can also generate ideas for social media content creation. By inputting your brand keywords and target audience information, ChatGPT can provide you with a list of potential content ideas, such as blog posts, infographics, videos, and images. You can then use these ideas to create engaging social media content that resonates with your audience.

Here are some ways ChatGPT can help with social media content:

● **Generating captions and hashtags:** ChatGPT can be used to generate captions for your social media posts, as well as relevant hashtags. Simply input your post's topic or image, and ChatGPT can provide suggestions for captions and hashtags that will resonate with your audience.

Example:

Input: Can you suggest a caption for this photo of a sunset?

Output: "There's nothing more beautiful than the colors of a sunset. 🌅 #sunsetlover #naturephotography #peacefulvibes"

- Brainstorming post ideas: Need help with what to post next? Use ChatGPT to generate ideas for your social media content. Input your brand or topic, and ChatGPT can provide suggestions for post ideas based on popular trends and topics.

Example:

Input: Can you suggest some post ideas for a fitness Instagram account?

Output: "5-minute workouts for busy schedules", "Healthy meal prep ideas," "The benefits of stretching before a workout"

- Creating social media ads: ChatGPT can also create effective social media ads. Input your target audience and campaign goal, and ChatGPT can provide suggestions for ad copy and imagery that will help you reach your target audience and drive conversions.

Example:

Input: Can you suggest ad copy for a social media campaign targeting millennials for a new skincare product?

Output: "Say goodbye to blemishes and hello to glowing skin! Our new skincare line is made with all-natural ingredients, perfect for sensitive skin. Try it out today and feel confident in your own skin! #skincare #allnatural #millennialbeauty"

3. **Social Media Advertising -** Social media advertising effectively reaches a wider audience and promotes your products or services. ChatGPT can be used to automate the process of creating social media

ads. By inputting your target audience information and ad objectives, ChatGPT can generate ad copy and design ideas. You can then use a social media advertising platform, such as Facebook Ads or Twitter Ads, to create and launch your ads.

ChatGPT can be used to generate ad copy for social media advertising campaigns. Ad copy is an advertisement's written content promoting a product or service. Therefore, it is essential to create compelling ad copy that captures the target audience's attention and entices them to take action. With ChatGPT, you can generate multiple ad copy variations and choose the best one for your campaign. Here are some ways to use ChatGPT in social media advertising:

a) **Generating Ad Headlines:** ChatGPT can generate headlines that are catchy and attention-grabbing. You can input a description of your product or service, and ChatGPT can generate various headlines highlighting the unique features and benefits of your product or service. For example, if you're advertising a fitness product, you could input "innovative workout equipment," and ChatGPT could generate headlines such as "Revolutionize Your Fitness Routine with Our Innovative Workout Equipment" or "Transform Your Body with the Latest Fitness Equipment."

b) **Creating Ad Descriptions:** ChatGPT can also generate ad descriptions that provide more information about your product or service. You can input your product or service's key features and benefits, and ChatGPT can generate descriptions highlighting those features and benefits. For example, if you're advertising a new mobile app, you could input "helps you stay organized," and ChatGPT could generate descriptions such as "Never forget a task again with our mobile app. Stay organized and on top of your to-do list wherever you go."

c) **Crafting Ad Copy Variations:** With ChatGPT, you can generate multiple ad copy variations for your social media advertising campaigns. By inputting different descriptions and features of your product or service, you can generate unique ad copy targeting different audience segments. For example, if you're advertising a beauty product, you could input "restores skin's natural glow" and "reduces the appearance of wrinkles" to generate ad copy that appeals to different customer needs.

d) **Optimizing Ad Copy:** ChatGPT can help you optimize your ad copy by analyzing the performance of your previous ads. By inputting the data from your previous ad campaigns, ChatGPT can generate new ad copy incorporating the elements that performed well in the past. For example, if your previous ad had a high click-through rate, ChatGPT could analyze the ad copy and generate new variations that incorporate the same language or phrases that resonated with your audience before.

e) **A/B Testing Ad Copy:** ChatGPT can generate ad copy variations for A/B testing. A/B testing is a method of testing different versions of an ad to see which one performs better. By generating multiple ad copy variations with ChatGPT, you can test different headlines, descriptions, and features to see which ones perform best. For example, you could generate two variations of an ad copy with different headlines and test them to see which one gets more clicks or conversions.

4. **Social Media Analytics** - Measuring the effectiveness of your social media campaigns is crucial for improving your strategy and maximizing your return on investment. ChatGPT can be used to analyze your social media analytics data and provide insights into the performance of your posts, ads, and campaigns. This can help you

identify what works and what doesn't and adjust your social media strategy accordingly.

ChatGPT can be a valuable tool for analyzing social media data and gaining insights into your audience's behavior and preferences. Here are some ways you can use ChatGPT in social media analytics:

- **Sentiment analysis:** ChatGPT can analyze the sentiment of social media posts and comments. This can help you understand how your audience feels about your brand and products and identify any issues that need to be addressed.

For example, let's say you own a clothing store and want to analyze the sentiment of social media posts about your brand. You could input a sample of posts into ChatGPT, and it would analyze the language used to determine whether the sentiment is positive, negative, or neutral.

- **Topic analysis:** ChatGPT can also be used to analyze the topics discussed on social media. This can help you identify trends and topics of interest to your audience and tailor your content accordingly.

For example, let's say you own a fitness company and want to identify the most popular topics related to fitness on social media. You could input a sample of social media posts into ChatGPT, and it would identify the most common topics being discussed, such as workout routines, nutrition, and motivation.

- **Influencer analysis:** ChatGPT can also be used to analyze the influence of social media influencers. This can help you identify which influencers are most effective at reaching your target audience and optimize your influencer marketing strategy.

For example, let's say you want to identify the most effective influencers in the beauty industry. You could input a list of influencers into ChatGPT, and it would analyze their social media engagement rates and audience demographics to identify the most effective influencers for your brand.

- **Audience analysis:** ChatGPT can also be used to analyze the demographics and behavior of your social media audience. This can help you tailor your content and advertising to reach your target audience better.

For example, let's say you want to analyze the demographics of your Instagram audience. You could input a sample of Instagram followers into ChatGPT, and it would analyze their age, gender, location, and other demographic information to help you better understand your audience.

5. **Social Media Influencer Marketing -** Influencer marketing is a popular way to promote products or services on social media. ChatGPT can identify potential social media influencers that align with your brand values and target audience. By inputting your brand keywords and target audience information, ChatGPT can generate a list of potential influencers you can contact and collaborate with.

Social media influencer marketing has become a popular way for brands to reach their target audience through influential individuals with a large social media following. ChatGPT can enhance the effectiveness of influencer marketing campaigns by providing insights and suggestions for content creation, audience targeting, and performance analysis.

Here are some ways to use ChatGPT in social media influencer marketing:

- **Audience Targeting:** ChatGPT can help identify the most relevant influencers for a brand's target audience. By analyzing data such as audience demographics, interests, and engagement rates, ChatGPT can suggest influencers with a high potential to reach the desired audience.

- Performance Analysis: ChatGPT can also be used to analyze the performance of influencer marketing campaigns. By inputting data such as engagement rates, click-through rates, and conversions,

ChatGPT can suggest areas for improvement and optimization. For instance, if a brand's influencer campaign is not generating the expected number of conversions, ChatGPT can suggest adjusting the messaging or targeting of the campaign.

- **Influencer Briefing:** ChatGPT can create an influencer briefing document that outlines the campaign objectives, messaging, and guidelines. By inputting information such as brand tone and voice, messaging objectives, and campaign goals, ChatGPT can generate a briefing document that can be shared with influencers. For example, if a company is launching a new line of eco-friendly products, ChatGPT can generate a briefing document emphasizing the importance of sustainability and eco-friendliness.

- **Influencer Outreach:** ChatGPT can also generate outreach messages to influencers. By inputting information such as the campaign objectives, influencer criteria, and desired outcomes, ChatGPT can suggest personalized and effective messaging in engaging with influencers. For instance, if a brand is looking to partner with micro-influencers in the beauty industry, ChatGPT can suggest messaging emphasizing the importance of authenticity and personal experience in promoting the brand.

6. **Social Media Monitoring -** Monitoring your brand's social media presence is important for managing your reputation and responding to customer feedback. ChatGPT can monitor social media mentions and keywords related to your brand. By inputting your brand keywords and target audience information, ChatGPT can provide you with real-time alerts on social media conversations that you should be aware of. This allows you to respond promptly and address any issues that arise.

Social media monitoring is the process of tracking online conversations to gain insights into customer sentiment and preferences, monitor brand reputation, and identify opportunities for engagement. It involves tracking mentions of your brand, competitors, and relevant keywords on social media platforms such as Facebook, Twitter, Instagram, LinkedIn, and others. ChatGPT can be a powerful tool for social media monitoring, as it can process large amounts of data. In this part, we will discuss how to use ChatGPT in social media monitoring.

a) Sentiment Analysis

One of the primary use cases of ChatGPT in social media monitoring is sentiment analysis. Sentiment analysis is the process of identifying the emotional tone of a piece of text, whether it is positive, negative, or neutral. Using ChatGPT, you can analyze the sentiment of social media posts and comments related to your brand or industry.

For example, let's say you run a clothing brand and want to track customer sentiment about your brand on social media. You can use ChatGPT to analyze the sentiment of social media posts and comments that mention your brand name, product name, or relevant keywords. ChatGPT can provide real-time insights into customer sentiment, allowing you to identify potential issues or opportunities for engagement.

b) Trend Analysis

Another use case of ChatGPT in social media monitoring is trend analysis. Trend analysis involves tracking the popularity of specific topics or keywords on social media platforms. Using ChatGPT, you can track the frequency and popularity of relevant keywords and topics, providing insights into emerging trends and conversations.

For example, let's say you run a technology company and want to track emerging trends in the industry. You can use ChatGPT to analyze the frequency and popularity of relevant keywords and topics on social media platforms, such as "artificial intelligence," "machine learning," and "big data." ChatGPT can provide real-time insights into emerging trends and conversations, allowing you to stay ahead of the curve.

c) Competitor Analysis

ChatGPT can also be used for competitor analysis in social media monitoring. By tracking mentions of your competitors on social media platforms, you can gain insights into their marketing strategies, customer sentiment, and potential opportunities for engagement.

For example, let's say you run a restaurant and want to track your competitors' mentions on social media platforms. You can use ChatGPT to analyze the frequency and sentiment of social media posts and comments that mention your competitors' names, products, or relevant keywords. As a result, ChatGPT can provide insights into your competitors' marketing strategies, allowing you to adjust your marketing efforts accordingly.

d) Influencer Identification

Influencer identification is another use case of ChatGPT in social media monitoring. Influencers are social media users with a significant following and influence over their followers. By identifying influencers in your industry or niche, you can leverage their influence to reach a broader audience and increase brand awareness.

For example, let's say you run a beauty brand and want to identify influencers in the beauty industry who can promote your products. You can use ChatGPT to analyze social media posts and comments related to beauty and identify users with a significant following and influence.

e) Crisis Management

Finally, ChatGPT can be used for crisis management in social media monitoring. In the event of a crisis or negative publicity, social media monitoring can help you identify potential issues early on and respond promptly and effectively. Using ChatGPT, you can monitor social media platforms for mentions of your brand and respond to them to address any concerns or issues.

Example: Let's say a customer posts a negative review on Twitter about your company's customer service. You can use ChatGPT to monitor Twitter for any mentions of your brand and identify the negative review. From there, you can use ChatGPT to generate a response acknowledging the customer's complaint, apologizing for any inconvenience, and offering a solution. This can help address the customer's concern and show other followers that your company takes customer service seriously and is willing to go above and beyond to ensure customer satisfaction.

By incorporating ChatGPT into your social media monitoring strategy, you can stay on top of social media trends and conversations, respond to customer feedback, and ultimately build a stronger online presence for your brand.

In conclusion, ChatGPT can be a valuable tool for generating passive income through social media management. By automating and enhancing your social media activities, you can save time and resources while also improving the effectiveness of your campaigns.

Digital products

Creating and promoting digital products can be a great way to generate passive income, and ChatGPT can be a valuable tool to aid in the process. In this section, we'll explore different types of digital products, how ChatGPT can be used to generate ideas and improve quality, and strategies for promoting and selling digital products.

TYPES OF DIGITAL PRODUCTS

Many types of digital products can be created, including:

1. **E-books:** E-books are digital versions of books that can be read on devices like e-readers, tablets, and smartphones. They can cover a wide range of topics, from fiction to self-help to business.

ChatGPT can help you generate content quickly and easily for e-books. Here are some steps to use ChatGPT to do so:

1) **Choose a topic:** Start by deciding on a topic for your e-book. Then, you can use ChatGPT to generate ideas by inputting keywords related to your niche and seeing what suggestions it generates.

2) **Create an outline:** Once you have a topic, use ChatGPT to generate an outline for your e-book. Input the topic and any related keywords, and see what suggestions ChatGPT generates. You can use these suggestions to create an outline for your e-book, which will help you organize your content.

3) **Generate content:** Use ChatGPT to generate content for your e-book. For example, input your outline or specific topics you want to cover, and let ChatGPT generate ideas and content for you. You can also use ChatGPT to refine your writing by suggesting synonyms, rephrasing sentences, and providing additional information.

4) **Edit and refine:** After generating the content, it's important to edit and refine it to ensure it's high-quality and error-free. Use ChatGPT to suggest edits and improvements and make any necessary changes yourself.

5) **Design and format:** Once you have your content, it's time to design and format your e-book. You can use tools like Canva or Adobe InDesign to create a professional-looking design. You can also use ChatGPT to generate ideas for the design and layout of your e-book.

6) **Publish and promote:** Finally, publish your e-book on platforms like Amazon Kindle or your own website, and promote it on social media and other channels. Use ChatGPT to generate ideas for promotional materials like blog posts, social media captions, and email campaigns.

By leveraging the capabilities of ChatGPT, you can create high-quality, unique content that provides value to readers and attracts a wide audience. With the right marketing strategy, your e-book can become a profitable source of passive income for years to come.

2. **Online courses:** Online courses are a popular type of digital product that offer in-depth education on a particular topic. They can include videos, written content, quizzes, and other interactive elements.

Creating online courses is a popular way of sharing knowledge and generating passive income. ChatGPT can be a useful tool in creating online courses by providing insights, ideas, and structure for course content.

Here are some steps on how to use ChatGPT to create online courses:

a) Define the Course Topic and Objectives:

The first step in creating an online course is to define the topic and objectives. What do you want your learners to know or be able to do after completing the course? Once you have defined the topic and objectives, input them into ChatGPT for further insights and ideas.

Example:

Input: I want to create an online course on digital marketing for beginners.

Output: The course should cover the basics of digital marketing, including SEO, social media marketing, email marketing, and paid advertising. The course's objectives should be to help learners understand the principles of digital marketing and how to create a digital marketing strategy.

b) Develop the Course Outline:

After defining the course topic and objectives, the next step is to develop the course outline. Again, inputting the course topic and objectives into ChatGPT can provide ideas for the structure and content of the course.

Example:

Input: Can you help me develop my digital marketing course outline?

Output: Introduction, Chapter 1: Understanding Digital Marketing, Chapter 2: Search Engine Optimization (SEO), Chapter 3: Social Media Marketing, Chapter 4: Email Marketing, Chapter 5: Paid Advertising, Chapter 6: Creating a Digital Marketing Strategy, Conclusion.

c) Generate Course Content:

Once you have developed the course outline, the next step is to generate the course content. ChatGPT can provide insights and ideas for each chapter or section of the course.

Example:

Input: Can you provide ideas for the SEO chapter of my digital marketing course?

Output: The SEO chapter should cover keyword research, on-page optimization, off-page optimization, and analytics. Learners should understand the importance of SEO for digital marketing and how to create an SEO strategy.

d) Refine and Edit Course Content:

After generating the course content, refining and editing it for clarity and accuracy is important. ChatGPT can suggest revisions and improvements to the course content.

Example:

Input: Can you help me refine the email marketing chapter of my course?

Output: The email marketing chapter should include email list building, segmentation, and automation information. Additionally, learners should understand how to write effective email copy and measure the success of their email campaigns.

e) Create Course Materials:

Once the course content is refined and edited, the next step is to create course materials such as video lectures, written lessons, and quizzes. ChatGPT can be used to provide ideas for the format and structure of the course materials.

Example:

Input: Can you provide ideas for the format of my digital marketing course videos?

Output: The videos should be engaging and informative, with clear and concise explanations of digital marketing concepts. Use examples and case studies to illustrate key points and make the content more relatable for learners.

f) Promote the Course:

Finally, once the course is created, it is important to promote it to potential learners. Again, chatGPT can be used to provide insights and ideas for course promotion and marketing.

Example:

Input: Can you provide ideas for promoting my digital marketing course?

Output: Promote the course through social media advertising, email marketing, and partnerships with other websites or influencers in the digital marketing space. Offer a free trial or demo of the course to attract new learners and generate interest.

3. **Software and apps:** Software and apps are digital products that offer a solution to a specific problem. They can be created for various desktop, mobile, and web platforms.

Creating software and apps can be a daunting task, but with the help of ChatGPT, you can streamline the process and create high-quality products.

Here's how you can use ChatGPT to create software and apps:

a) **Idea Generation:** The first step in creating software or an app is coming up with an idea. ChatGPT can help you brainstorm ideas by generating a list of potential concepts based on keywords and phrases that you input. For example:

Input: "Ideas for a new mobile app."

Output: "A fitness tracking app, a recipe app, a language learning app, a travel planner app, a music streaming app, a weather app, a productivity app, a photo editing app, a shopping app."

b) **Design and User Experience:** Once you have an idea, you need to design the user interface and experience. ChatGPT can help you by generating design suggestions and best practices based on industry standards and user behavior. For example:

Input: "Design tips for mobile app user interface."

Output: "Use a consistent color scheme, simplify navigation, minimize the use of text, provide clear calls to action, use high-quality images, design for different screen sizes, optimize for touch screens."

c) **Development:** After designing the user interface and experience, you need to develop the software or app. ChatGPT can help you by suggesting programming languages, libraries, and frameworks based on the type of software or app you want to create. For example:

Input: "Suggestions for programming languages for mobile app development."

Output: "Java, Kotlin, Swift, React Native, Xamarin, Ionic, Flutter, PhoneGap."

d) **Testing and Debugging:** Once the software or app is developed, it must be tested and debugged. ChatGPT can help you by suggesting testing frameworks and best practices based on the type of software or app you created. For example:

Input: "Testing frameworks for mobile app development."

Output: "JUnit, Espresso, Appium, Selenium, XCTest, KIF, Calabash."

    e) **Marketing and Promotion:** Once the software or app is ready, you need to market and promote it to reach your target audience. ChatGPT can help you by suggesting marketing strategies, keywords, and target demographics based on industry trends and user behavior. For example:

Input: "Marketing strategies for a new mobile app."

Output: "Social media advertising, influencer marketing, email marketing, app store optimization, search engine optimization, content marketing, word of mouth marketing."

Examples of using ChatGPT to create software and apps:

    1) **Creating a Language Learning App:** Let's say you want to create a language learning app. Here's an example of how you can use ChatGPT to generate ideas and suggestions:

Input: "Ideas for a language learning app."

Output: "A vocabulary builder, a grammar quiz, a conversation practice tool, a pronunciation trainer, a reading comprehension app, a listening comprehension app."

    2) **Creating a Weather App:** Let's say you want to create a weather app. Here's an example of how you can use ChatGPT to generate ideas and refine your app's features:

Input: Can you help me brainstorm features for a weather app?

Output: Sure! Some possible features include current temperature, hourly and daily forecasts, radar maps, severe weather alerts, customizable locations, and a user-friendly interface. Consider adding additional features such as pollen count, UV index, and air quality index.

Input: Can you suggest ways to improve the user experience of a weather app?

Output: Yes, here are some suggestions for improving the user experience: make it easy to navigate and understand, use simple and clear language, provide visual cues to help users understand the information, allow for customization, provide push notifications for severe weather alerts, and ensure that the app is responsive and fast.

ChatGPT can help you generate new ideas and refine your app's features to make it stand out in a competitive market.

4. **Graphic designs:** Graphic designs can include a wide range of products, such as logos, business cards, website templates, and social media graphics.

ChatGPT can also generate ideas and inspiration for graphic design projects. By inputting specific parameters and preferences, ChatGPT can provide a range of options and suggestions for different design elements.

Here are some steps to use ChatGPT to create graphic designs:

a) **Define your design parameters:** Before starting, it's important to define your design parameters, such as the dimensions, colors, fonts, and overall style of your design. This will help ChatGPT generate more relevant suggestions.

b) **Input your design preferences:** Once you have your parameters in mind, you can input your design preferences into ChatGPT. For example, you could ask for suggestions on a color palette that works well for a particular project or font options that complement a certain style.

c) **Evaluate the suggestions:** After inputting your preferences, ChatGPT will provide a range of options and suggestions for different design elements. Evaluating these suggestions and choosing the ones that align with your vision for the project is important.

d) **Refine and iterate:** Once you've selected some initial design elements, you can use ChatGPT to refine and iterate your design. For example, you could input specific design elements you'd like to see incorporated, such as a certain type of image or graphic. Then, ChatGPT can generate suggestions based on these inputs.

e) **Implement and finalize:** After refining your design with ChatGPT, it's time to implement and finalize your design. You can use the suggestions provided by ChatGPT as a starting point and then make adjustments and tweaks as needed to create a final product that aligns with your vision.

Here are some examples of how ChatGPT can be used to generate design ideas:

1) **Logo Design:** Let's say you're creating a logo for a new company. You can input the company's name and any design preferences, such as preferred colors or style, and ChatGPT can generate a range of logo design options.

Input: "Create a logo for a new company called Blue Ocean. The logo should be simple and modern, with blue and green as the primary colors."

Output: ChatGPT could generate a range of logo designs with blue and green as the primary colors and with a modern and simple design.

2) **Website Design:** ChatGPT can generate ideas and inspiration for website design projects. By inputting specific design parameters and preferences, ChatGPT can provide a range of options for different design elements, such as layout, color scheme, and font choice.

Input: "I need a website design for a new fashion brand. The website should have a clean and modern look, with a black and white color scheme and a focus on high-quality images."

Output: ChatGPT could generate various website designs with a black-and-white color scheme and a focus on high-quality images, with different layout options and font choices.

3) **Social Media Graphics:** Social media graphics are an important part of any online marketing strategy, and ChatGPT can be used to generate ideas and inspiration for different types of social media graphics, such as posts, banners, and ads.

Input: "I need a social media graphic for an upcoming sale. The graphic should be eye-catching and include the sale dates and discount code."

Output: ChatGPT could generate a range of social media graphics with different design elements, such as bold fonts, bright colors, and images of sale items, to help create an eye-catching and effective graphic for the upcoming sale.

5. **Music and audio files:** Music and audio files can be sold as digital downloads, including songs, sound effects, and audiobooks.

Creating music and audio files is an art form that can take years of practice and skill development. While ChatGPT cannot replace the expertise of a musician or audio engineer, it can be a useful tool for generating ideas and providing inspiration for new compositions.

Here are some ways that ChatGPT can be used to create music and audio files:

- **Generating lyrics:** ChatGPT can be used to generate lyrics for a song. By providing the model with a topic or theme, it can generate lines of text that can be used as a starting point for songwriting. For example:

Input: Can you generate some lyrics for a love song?

Output: "When I'm with you, I feel alive. Every moment we share feels like we can survive. You're the light in my darkness, the hope that I need. My heart beats for you, my love, indeed."

- **Creating melody ideas:** ChatGPT can also be used to create melody ideas for a composition. By inputting chord progressions or musical ideas, it can generate melody lines to be used as a starting point for a new composition. For example:

Input: Can you generate a melody based on the chord progression Am - F - C - G?

Output: [Melody audio file]

- **Providing sound effects:** ChatGPT can generate sound effects for audio files. By inputting keywords or phrases that describe the desired sound, it can generate audio files for music compositions or audio productions. For example:

Input: Can you generate a sound effect of a thunderstorm?

Output: [Thunderstorm sound effect audio file]

- **Generating ambient music:** ChatGPT can generate ambient music for background soundscapes. By inputting keywords or themes, it can generate ambient music for video productions, relaxation soundscapes, and more. For example:

Input: Can you generate ambient music for a forest soundscape?

Output: [Forest soundscape audio file]

- **Remixing existing audio files:** ChatGPT can be used to remix existing audio files. By inputting audio files and providing guidelines for the desired remix, it can generate new audio files incorporating elements of the original audio file. For example:

Input: Can you remix this audio file to include more percussion elements?

Output: [Remixed audio file]

ChatGPT can be a useful tool for generating ideas and providing inspiration for music and audio production. However, it should be noted that the final product will require the expertise and skills of a trained musician or audio engineer to ensure that it meets industry standards and sounds professional.

STRATEGIES FOR PROMOTING AND SELLING DIGITAL PRODUCTS THROUGH CHATGPT

With the rise of technology and the internet, digital products have become more prevalent. Digital products are essentially anything that can be delivered electronically, such as software, e-books, courses, and more. Selling these products can be incredibly lucrative, but getting the word out and attracting customers can also be challenging. ChatGPT can be an effective tool for promoting and selling digital products. This part will explore some strategies for using ChatGPT to market and sell digital products.

1) Provide High-Quality Content

The first step in promoting and selling digital products through ChatGPT is to create high-quality content that your audience will find valuable. This could be in the form of blog posts, e-books, whitepapers, or any other digital content your target market is interested in. The key is to provide informative, engaging, and relevant content to your audience.

When you create high-quality content, you establish yourself as an authority in your niche. This can help build trust with your audience and make it easier to sell your digital products. For example, if you sell an online course on digital marketing, you could create a series of blog posts that cover different aspects of digital marketing. These posts would provide value to your audience and establish your expertise in the field, making it more likely that they will purchase your course.

2) Use ChatGPT to Build Relationships with Your Audience

One of the benefits of using ChatGPT to promote and sell digital products is that it allows you to build relationships with your audience. Chatbots can be programmed to engage in conversation with users, providing them with information and answering their questions. This can help establish a connection with your audience and make them more likely to purchase your digital products.

To use ChatGPT effectively, it's important to personalize your conversations with your audience. Instead of sending generic messages, try to tailor your messages to the individual user. For example, if a user asks a question about a specific aspect of your digital product, you could provide them with a personalized response addressing their concerns.

3) Use ChatGPT to Offer Discounts and Promotions

Another effective way to use ChatGPT to promote and sell digital products is to offer discounts and promotions. Chatbots can be programmed to send users personalized discount codes and promotions, encouraging them to make a purchase. This can be a powerful way to increase sales and attract new customers.

When offering discounts and promotions, it's important to create a sense of urgency. For example, you could offer a limited-time discount or a special promotion that is only available to users who purchase within a certain time frame. This can encourage users to make a purchase sooner rather than later.

4) Use ChatGPT to Provide Support

Another way to use ChatGPT to promote and sell digital products is to provide support to your customers. Chatbots can be programmed to provide users with information and support related to your digital products. This can be incredibly valuable for users who may have questions or concerns about your products.

By providing support through ChatGPT, you can ensure your customers have a positive experience with your digital products. This can help build trust and make it more likely that they will purchase from you in the future.

5) Use ChatGPT to Gather Feedback

Finally, you can use ChatGPT to gather feedback from your customers. Chatbots can be programmed to ask users for feedback on your products, which can help you identify areas for improvement. This can be valuable for improving your digital products and ensuring your customers' satisfaction with their purchases.

When gathering feedback, it's important to ask specific questions that will provide you with actionable insights. For example, you could ask users what they liked and didn't like about your product, or you could ask them if they would recommend your product to others. You can also ask open-ended questions that allow users to provide more detailed feedback.

Once you have gathered feedback, it's important to take action on the insights you have gained. For example, if users consistently provide negative feedback about a certain aspect of your product, you may need to make changes to address those concerns. On the other hand, if users are consistently providing positive feedback about a certain aspect of your product, you should highlight that feature more prominently in your marketing materials.

ChatGPT can be an effective tool for promoting and selling digital products. By providing high-quality content, building relationships with your audience, offering discounts and promotions, providing support, and gathering feedback, you can use ChatGPT to increase sales and attract new customers. However, it's important to remember that ChatGPT should be part of a larger marketing strategy. In order to be successful, you need to clearly understand your target market, your value proposition, and your overall marketing goals. Combining ChatGPT with other marketing strategies can create a comprehensive approach that drives sales and grows your business.

VII. BECOME A SUPERHUMAN FREELANCER WITH CHATGPT

Freelancing has become an increasingly popular way for people to work in recent years. With the rise of the gig economy and technological advances, it's now easier than ever to work for yourself and earn a living on your own terms. However, freelancing can be a challenging and competitive field, and it's important to have the right tools and strategies in place to succeed. In this chapter, we'll explore how ChatGPT can help you become a superhuman freelancer by improving your productivity, expanding your skills, and enhancing your communication with clients.

EXPANDING YOUR SERVICE OFFERINGS

As a business owner or service provider, it's essential to offer your clients a wide range of services. However, developing and expanding your service offering can take time and effort, especially if you're working with limited resources. Fortunately, with the help of ChatGPT, you can expand your service offering cost-effectively and efficiently. In this part, we'll explore how ChatGPT can help you expand your service offering by providing you with valuable insights, automating routine tasks, and enhancing your communication with clients.

Aside from data analysis, customer feedback, market research, social media management, and scheduling, ChatGPt can also help you in the following activities to expand your service offerings:

DEVELOPING NEW SERVICE OFFERINGS

Skill Development: ChatGPT can help you develop new skills that will enable you to expand your service offerings, such as coding, design, or copywriting.

In today's rapidly changing world, developing new skills to stay competitive in the workplace is essential. With the help of technology, skill development has become more accessible than ever before. One of the most effective tools for skill development is ChatGPT, an AI-based language model that can assist individuals in developing new skills in various fields.

These are some ways to use ChatGPT to help with skill development

1) Identifying the Skills to Develop

The first step in skill development is identifying the skills you want to develop. This could be based on your current job or industry or a skill you've always wanted to learn. Once you've identified the skill, you can research the best resources to help you develop it. ChatGPT can be a valuable resource in this process, as it can help you identify the most relevant and up-to-date resources for your skill development.

2) Creating a Learning Plan

Once you've identified the skills you want to develop, it's essential to create a learning plan. This plan should outline your goals, the resources you'll use, and the timeline for completing the skill development. ChatGPT can assist in this process by providing personalized recommendations for resources and helping you create a timeline for your learning plan.

3) Learning the Skill

Once you've created a learning plan, it's time to start learning the skill. ChatGPT can assist in this process by providing you with access to relevant courses, tutorials, and articles on the skill you're developing. It can also help you create a personalized learning experience by suggesting resources based on your learning style and preferences.

4) Practicing the Skill

Learning a skill is only the first step. To truly develop your skills, you need to practice them regularly. ChatGPT can assist in this process by providing you with opportunities to practice your skills in a simulated environment. For example, if you're developing your coding skills, ChatGPT can provide you with a coding environment to practice in, complete with real-time feedback and suggestions.

5) Tracking Your Progress

To ensure that you're progressing in your skill development, it's important to track your progress regularly. ChatGPT can assist in this process by providing you with regular progress reports and feedback on your performance. It can also help you identify areas where you need to improve and suggest resources to help you overcome any challenges you may be facing.

6) Networking and Collaboration

Networking and collaboration are essential for skill development. ChatGPT can assist in this process by connecting you with other individuals who are developing the same skill or working in the same industry. It can also help you form study groups, attend virtual events, and connect with mentors to help you accelerate your skill development.

In conclusion, ChatGPT can be a valuable tool for skill development. By assisting in identifying skills, creating learning plans, providing personalized recommendations, offering opportunities to practice, tracking progress, and connecting individuals, ChatGPT can help individuals achieve their career goals and stay competitive in the ever-changing job market.

SCALING YOUR SERVICE OFFERING

Outsourcing: ChatGPT can help you identify areas where you can outsource tasks or services to other service providers, allowing you to scale your business without incurring additional overhead costs.

Outsourcing has recently become a popular business practice as companies look to reduce costs and improve efficiency. However, finding the right outsourcing partner can be challenging.

Outsourcing can be a complex process involving many different stakeholders and decisions. ChatGPT can be used to support outsourcing in several ways:

- **Vendor selection:** ChatGPT can be trained on a specific data set, such as vendor performance metrics, to identify potential outsourcing partners. By analyzing vendor performance data, ChatGPT can identify vendors with a track record of success in a particular industry or region.

- **Request for Proposal (RFP) development:** ChatGPT can be used to develop RFPs for outsourcing projects. By analyzing existing RFPs and best practices, ChatGPT can generate a customized RFP that meets the needs of the business and provides clear expectations for potential vendors.

- **Contract negotiation:** ChatGPT can support contract negotiations by analyzing contract language and identifying potential areas of concern. By providing insights into potential risks and opportunities, ChatGPT can help businesses negotiate more favorable outsourcing contracts.

- **Performance monitoring:** ChatGPT can monitor outsourcing partners' performance by analyzing performance metrics and providing real-time insights into potential issues. By identifying potential problems early on, ChatGPT can help businesses take corrective action before they become major issues.

- **Knowledge management:** ChatGPT can be used to support knowledge management by analyzing existing documentation and creating a centralized repository of information. By providing easy access to information, ChatGPT can help businesses make more informed outsourcing decisions and streamline their processes.

CASE STUDY: USING CHATGPT FOR VENDOR SELECTION

One example of how ChatGPT can be used for outsourcing is vendor selection. A large multinational corporation was looking to outsource its IT services to a third-party provider. However, with so many potential vendors, the company struggled to identify the right partner for their needs.

The company used ChatGPT to analyze vendor performance data from various sources, including customer feedback, industry reports, and internal performance metrics, to support its vendor selection process. By training ChatGPT on this data, the company was able to identify vendors with a track record of success in their industry and region.

The company also used ChatGPT to generate a customized RFP that provided clear expectations for potential vendors and helped streamline the bidding process. In addition, by providing real-time insights into vendor performance, ChatGPT helped the company monitor vendor performance and identify potential issues early on.

Whether you're looking to outsource IT services, customer support, or other operations, ChatGPT can provide the support you need to find the right partner for your needs.

Strategic Partnerships: ChatGPT can help you form strategic partnerships with other businesses and service providers, allowing you to offer your clients more comprehensive and integrated services.

Strategic partnerships are critical for the success of any business. By working with other companies, businesses can leverage each other's strengths to achieve common goals. However, identifying and building strategic partnerships can be complex and require careful planning and execution. This section will explore how businesses can use ChatGPT to build strategic partnerships and achieve their business goals.

CHATGPT AND STRATEGIC PARTNERSHIPS

Strategic partnerships are partnerships between two or more companies that work together to achieve common goals. Building these partnerships can be a complex process that involves identifying potential partners, assessing their strengths and weaknesses, and developing a plan for collaboration. ChatGPT can be used to support the process of building strategic partnerships in several ways:

1) **Partner identification:** ChatGPT can be trained on a specific data set, such as industry reports or market research, to identify potential partners. ChatGPT can identify companies with complementary strengths and a shared vision by analyzing this data.

2) **Partner assessment:** ChatGPT can assess potential partners by analyzing their performance metrics, financial data, and customer feedback. ChatGPT can help businesses make informed decisions about who to partner with by providing real-time insights into potential partners.

3) **Collaboration planning:** ChatGPT can be used to develop a plan for collaboration by analyzing the goals and objectives of each partner and identifying areas of overlap. By providing real-time insights into potential challenges and opportunities, ChatGPT can help businesses develop a collaborative plan that maximizes the strengths of each partner.

4) **Communication support:** ChatGPT can support communication between partners by providing real-time translation and analysis of messages. ChatGPT can help partners build stronger relationships and work more effectively together by facilitating communication.

CASE STUDY: USING CHATGPT IN BUILDING STRATEGIC PARTNERSHIPS

One example of how ChatGPT can be used to build strategic partnerships is the healthcare industry. A large hospital system was looking to build a strategic partnership with a medical device company to improve patient outcomes and reduce costs.

To support their partnership-building process, the hospital system used ChatGPT to analyze industry reports and identify potential partners with a track record of success in medical device development. By training ChatGPT on this data, the hospital system was able to identify a shortlist of potential partners that shared their vision for improving patient outcomes.

The hospital system also used ChatGPT to assess potential partners by analyzing their performance metrics and customer feedback. ChatGPT helped the hospital system make an informed decision about who to partner with by providing real-time insights into potential partners.

Finally, the hospital system used ChatGPT to develop a collaborative plan with their chosen partner that maximized the strengths of each organization. By providing real-time insights into potential challenges and opportunities, ChatGPT helped the partners build a plan that would achieve their common goals.

ChatGPT can be a valuable tool for businesses looking to build strategic partnerships. Whether you're looking to build a partnership in healthcare, finance, or another industry, ChatGPT can provide the support you need to achieve your business goals.

Expanding your service offering through ChatGPT is all about leveraging the power of technology to work smarter, not harder. With the help of ChatGPT, the possibilities for expanding your service offering are endless.

INCREASING EFFICIENCY AND PRODUCTIVITY

Efficiency and productivity are critical to the success of any business. Businesses can achieve better results, increase revenue, and gain a competitive advantage by optimizing processes and increasing output. However, identifying and implementing improvements can be a complex process that requires careful planning and execution. This part will explore how businesses can use ChatGPT to increase efficiency and productivity.

CHATGPT AND EFFICIENCY

Efficiency refers to the ability of a business to accomplish tasks with the least amount of time and resources possible. Increasing efficiency can result in cost savings, increased output, and improved customer satisfaction. ChatGPT can be used to support the process of increasing efficiency in several ways:

1) **Process optimization:** ChatGPT can be used to analyze existing processes and identify opportunities for optimization. By training ChatGPT on data from process documentation or customer feedback, businesses can identify areas where processes can be streamlined or automated.

2) **Real-time analysis:** ChatGPT can provide real-time analysis of data and processes. By analyzing data, ChatGPT can identify potential issues or opportunities for improvement and alert relevant stakeholders.

3) **Predictive analysis:** ChatGPT can provide predictive analysis of potential outcomes. By analyzing data from past performance, ChatGPT can provide insights into potential outcomes and help businesses make informed decisions about future actions.

ChatGPT and Productivity

Productivity refers to the ability of a business to produce a certain amount of output with a given amount of inputs. Increasing productivity can result in increased revenue and profitability. ChatGPT can be used to support the process of increasing productivity in several ways:

1) **Process automation:** ChatGPT can be used to automate routine tasks and free up time for more complex tasks. By training ChatGPT on data from existing processes, businesses can identify areas where automation can be implemented.

2) **Real-time support:** ChatGPT can be used to provide real-time support to employees. By providing employees with quick and accurate responses to their questions, ChatGPT can help them work more efficiently and productively.

3) **Knowledge management:** ChatGPT can capture and share knowledge across the organization. By training ChatGPT on data from existing documentation or employee knowledge, businesses can create a centralized knowledge base that employees can access to increase productivity.

Case Study: Using ChatGPT to Increase Efficiency and Productivity

One example of how ChatGPT can increase efficiency and productivity is the retail industry. A large retail chain sought to optimize its inventory management processes to reduce waste and increase revenue.

To support their process optimization efforts, the retail chain used ChatGPT to analyze customer feedback and identify opportunities for improvement. By training ChatGPT on this data, the retail chain was able to identify patterns in customer behavior and optimize its inventory management processes to reduce waste and increase revenue.

The retail chain also used ChatGPT to automate routine tasks like inventory tracking and ordering. By training ChatGPT on data from existing processes, the retail chain was able to automate these tasks and free up time for employees to focus on more complex tasks.

Finally, the retail chain used ChatGPT to capture and share knowledge across the organization. By training ChatGPT on data from existing documentation and employee knowledge, the retail chain was able to create a centralized knowledge base that employees could access to increase productivity.

STANDING OUT IN THE MARKETPLACE

In today's crowded marketplace, it can be challenging for businesses to stand out and differentiate themselves from competitors. However, standing out is essential for success, as it can help businesses attract and retain customers, increase revenue, and gain a competitive advantage.

These are some strategies that can help your business stand out:

1. Know Your Target Audience

The first step to standing out in the marketplace is understanding your target audience. This includes knowing their needs, preferences, and pain points. Understanding your target audience allows you to tailor your messaging and marketing efforts to resonate with them.

One way to gain insight into your target audience is through market research. This can include surveys, focus groups, and other forms of feedback. By gathering feedback from your target audience, you can gain valuable insights into what they value and how they perceive your brand.

Here are some ways to use ChatGPT to know your target audience:

1. Conduct Market Research

ChatGPT can be used to conduct market research and gather valuable insights about your target audience. For example, you can use the tool to analyze customer feedback and social media conversations to identify common themes, pain points, and trends. This can help you better understand your target audience's needs and preferences and develop messaging that speaks directly to them.

2. Personalize Messaging

ChatGPT can create personalized messaging that resonates with your target audience. ChatGPT can help you identify common characteristics and preferences among your target audience by analyzing customer data and behavior. Then, you can use this information to create messaging that speaks directly to their interests and needs and deliver personalized experiences that enhance engagement and build loyalty.

3. Create Buyer Personas

ChatGPT can be used to create detailed buyer personas that capture your target audience's characteristics, preferences, and behaviors. ChatGPT can help you identify common patterns and trends among your target audience and create personas that reflect their unique needs and preferences by analyzing customer data and feedback. These personas can then be used to inform marketing strategies and personalize messaging that resonates with each segment of your target audience.

4. Identify Content Topics

ChatGPT can be used to identify content topics that resonate with your target audience. ChatGPT can help you identify common themes and topics of interest among your target audience by analyzing customer feedback and social media conversations. Then, you can use this information to create content that addresses their needs and interests and engage with them meaningfully.

5. Predict Customer Behavior

ChatGPT can be used to predict customer behavior and anticipate their needs. ChatGPT can help you identify patterns and trends that may indicate future actions or preferences by analyzing customer data and behavior. You can use this information to create targeted marketing campaigns and deliver personalized experiences that enhance engagement and build loyalty.

6. Analyze Customer Feedback

ChatGPT can be used to analyze customer feedback and identify common themes and issues. By analyzing customer reviews, feedback forms, and social media conversations, ChatGPT can help you identify areas for improvement and develop strategies to address them. This can help you improve the customer experience and build loyalty among your target audience.

2. Differentiate Your Brand

Differentiating your brand is essential for standing out in the marketplace. This means identifying what makes your brand unique and emphasizing those qualities in your messaging and marketing efforts.

One way to differentiate your brand is through branding. This includes your brand name, logo, colors, and other visual elements. Creating a distinctive brand identity can make your brand more memorable and recognizable.

Another way to differentiate your brand is through your product or service offering. This can include unique features or benefits that set your products or services apart from competitors. By emphasizing these unique qualities, you can make your brand more attractive to customers.

ChatGPT can be a valuable tool for differentiating your brand and standing out in a crowded marketplace. Using the tool to analyze customer data, market trends, and industry insights, you can gain valuable insights into what sets your brand apart and develop messaging that speaks directly to your target audience.

Here are some ways to use ChatGPT to differentiate your brand:

a) Identify Unique Selling Points

ChatGPT can be used to identify the unique selling points of your brand. ChatGPT can help you identify the key features and benefits that set your brand apart from competitors by analyzing customer feedback, market trends, and industry insights. You can then use this information to develop messaging that emphasizes these unique selling points and highlights the value of your brand to your target audience.

b) Develop a Unique Voice and Tone

ChatGPT can be used to develop a unique voice and tone for your brand. ChatGPT can help you identify the language and communication style that resonates with your target audience by analyzing customer data and feedback. You can then use this information to develop messaging that speaks directly to their interests and needs and creates a distinctive brand voice that sets you apart from competitors.

c) Create a Brand Personality

ChatGPT can create a brand personality that resonates with your target audience. By analyzing customer data and feedback, Chat GPT can help you identify the traits and characteristics your target audience values in a brand. You can then use this information to develop a brand personality that reflects these values and creates an emotional connection with your target audience.

d) Develop a Unique Brand Story

ChatGPT can be used to develop a unique brand story that sets your brand apart from competitors. ChatGPT can help you identify the key themes and values that resonate with your target audience by analyzing market trends and industry insights. You can then use this information to develop a brand story that emphasizes your unique selling points and creates a compelling narrative that resonates with your target audience.

e) Differentiate Your Brand Visuals

ChatGPT can be used to differentiate your brand visuals and create a distinctive visual identity. Chat GPT can help you identify the visual elements that resonate with your target audience by analyzing customer data and feedback. You can then use this information to develop a visual identity that reflects your unique brand personality and creates a distinctive visual presence that sets you apart from competitors.

f) Personalize Messaging

ChatGPT can personalize messaging and create a personalized experience for your target audience. ChatGPT can help you identify common characteristics and preferences among your target audience by analyzing customer data and behavior. You can then use this information to create messaging that speaks directly to their interests and needs and deliver personalized experiences that enhance engagement and build loyalty.

3. Build a Strong Brand Reputation

Building a strong brand reputation is essential for standing out in the marketplace. This means developing a reputation for reliability, quality, and innovation.

One way to build a strong brand reputation is to deliver high-quality products and services consistently. This can help build trust and loyalty among your customers, who will more likely recommend your brand to others.

Another way to build a strong brand reputation is to engage in corporate social responsibility (CSR) activities. This can include supporting charitable causes, implementing eco-friendly practices, or engaging in community outreach efforts. Demonstrating a commitment to social and environmental issues can enhance your brand's reputation and appeal to socially conscious customers.

A strong brand reputation is essential for the long-term success of any business. ChatGPT can be a valuable tool for building and managing a strong brand reputation by analyzing customer feedback, monitoring industry trends, and providing insights into brand perception.

Here are some ways to use ChatGPT in building a strong brand reputation:

1) Monitor Brand Mentions

ChatGPT can be used to monitor brand mentions across social media platforms and other online channels. By analyzing customer feedback, ChatGPT can provide real-time insights into how customers perceive your brand and identify potential issues that could impact your reputation. You can then use this information to address concerns and respond to customer feedback promptly and effectively.

2) Identify Key Influencers

ChatGPT can be used to identify key influencers in your industry or niche. By analyzing social media data and other online channels, ChatGPT can identify individuals or groups who significantly impact your target audience's perceptions of your brand. You can then use this information to engage with these influencers and build relationships that can help strengthen your brand reputation.

3) Develop a Crisis Management Plan

ChatGPT can be used to develop a crisis management plan to help mitigate potential reputation risks. By analyzing customer feedback and industry trends, ChatGPT can help you identify potential issues impacting your brand reputation and develop a plan to address them proactively. This can help you minimize the impact of negative events and protect your brand reputation over the long term.

4) Use Social Listening to Understand Customer Sentiment

ChatGPT can be used to monitor customer sentiment across social media platforms and other online channels. By analyzing customer feedback, ChatGPT can help you identify areas where your brand is performing well and where improvements may be needed. You can then use this information to make data-driven decisions that help strengthen your brand reputation.

5) Develop Brand Guidelines

ChatGPT can be used to develop brand guidelines that ensure consistent messaging and visual identity across all marketing channels. By analyzing customer feedback and industry trends, ChatGPT can help you identify the key elements that define your brand identity. You can then use this information to develop brand guidelines that align all marketing efforts with your brand values and messaging.

6) Personalize Brand Interactions

ChatGPT can be used to personalize brand interactions with customers, which can help build brand loyalty and strengthen your reputation. ChatGPT can help you identify common characteristics and preferences among your target audience by analyzing customer data and behavior. You can then use this information to create personalized experiences that enhance engagement and build loyalty.

4. Provide Value-Added Services

Providing value-added services can be a powerful way to stand out in the marketplace. This means offering additional services or benefits that go above and beyond what customers might expect.

One way to provide value-added services is to offer free or discounted add-ons with your products or services. For example, a restaurant might offer a free appetizer with a meal, or a car dealership might offer a free oil change with the purchase of a new car.

Another way to provide value-added services is to offer educational resources or support. This can include online tutorials or training sessions that help customers get the most out of your products or services.

145

ChatGPT can provide value-added services to customers by facilitating personalized, efficient, and responsive interactions. Here are some ways to use ChatGPT to provide value-added services:

1) **Personalization**

ChatGPT can personalize customer interactions by analyzing data on their past interactions, preferences, and behaviors. Using natural language processing, ChatGPT can generate personalized responses to customer queries, recommend products or services based on past behavior, and tailor offers and promotions to their interests.

2) **Efficiency**

ChatGPT can be used to provide efficient customer service by automating responses to frequently asked questions, providing instant feedback on order status, and resolving issues quickly and effectively. Using ChatGPT, businesses can reduce the time and resources needed to handle customer inquiries and free up staff to focus on more complex tasks.

3) **Responsiveness**

ChatGPT can provide responsive customer service by enabling 24/7 availability and real-time response to customer queries. Using ChatGPT, businesses can ensure that customers are always on time to respond and that issues are resolved as quickly as possible.

4) **Proactive Support**

ChatGPT can be used to provide proactive support to customers by identifying potential issues before they occur and providing proactive guidance on how to avoid them. By analyzing customer data and identifying patterns and trends, ChatGPT can alert customers to potential issues, recommend solutions, and provide guidance on preventing similar issues in the future.

5) Upselling and Cross-selling

ChatGPT can be used to provide value-added services by recommending products or services that are relevant to the customer's needs and preferences. By analyzing customer data and past interactions, ChatGPT can identify opportunities for upselling or cross-selling and provide personalized recommendations to customers.

In conclusion, standing out in the marketplace requires a combination of strategies and tactics. By understanding your target audience, differentiating your brand, providing excellent customer service, using social media to your advantage, focusing on quality, innovating and adapting, building a strong brand reputation, collaborating with other businesses, providing value-added services, and being authentic and transparent, you can create a strong brand identity that resonates with customers and helps you stand out from the competition.

VIII. CONCLUSION

THE FUTURE OF AI AND CHATGPT

The future of AI and ChatGPT is incredibly exciting, and it is clear that these technologies will continue to play a significant role in transforming a wide range of industries in the future. Here are some trends that are likely to shape the future of AI and ChatGPT:

1. Greater Personalization

As AI and ChatGPT become more advanced, they will enable businesses to provide even more personalized customer experiences. By analyzing vast amounts of data on customer behavior, preferences, and habits, AI and ChatGPT will be able to provide highly tailored recommendations, content, and interactions that resonate with individual customers.

2. Improved Natural Language Processing

As the technology behind natural language processing continues to improve, ChatGPT will become even better at understanding and generating human-like responses. This will enable more seamless interactions between humans and machines, making it easier for people to get the information and support they need.

3. More Advanced Automation

AI and ChatGPT will continue revolutionizing how businesses operate, enabling greater automation of routine tasks and freeing employees to focus on more strategic work. This will increase efficiency, productivity, and profitability for businesses across various industries.

4. Greater Integration with IoT

As the Internet of Things (IoT) becomes more widespread, AI and ChatGPT will play an increasingly important role in helping businesses to collect, analyze, and act on the vast amounts of data generated by connected devices. This will enable businesses to make more informed decisions and create new products and services that meet the evolving needs of their customers.

5. Increased Use in Healthcare

AI and ChatGPT are already being used in various healthcare applications, from diagnosis and treatment planning to patient monitoring and drug development. As the technology continues to improve, we can expect to see even more applications of AI and Chat GPT in healthcare, helping to improve patient outcomes and reduce costs.

With greater personalization, improved natural language processing, more advanced automation, greater integration with IoT, and increased use in healthcare, the potential applications of AI and ChatGPT are truly limitless. As a result, businesses that invest in these technologies now are likely to reap significant benefits in the years to come.

STAYING AHEAD OF THE CURVE

To stay ahead of the curve, businesses need to be proactive in their approach to these technologies. Here are some strategies that businesses can use to stay ahead of the curve:

1. Keep up with Industry Trends

Businesses must stay informed about the latest developments in AI and ChatGPT by keeping up with industry trends and attending conferences and events. This will enable businesses to understand the potential applications of these technologies and stay ahead of the curve.

2. Invest in R&D

Businesses that invest in research and development in AI and ChatGPT are more likely to stay ahead of the curve. This involves identifying areas where

AI and ChatGPT can be used to improve operations, creating prototypes, and testing and refining these solutions until they are ready for implementation.

3. Partner with Tech Experts

Partnering with tech experts such as AI and ChatGPT developers can help businesses stay ahead of the curve. These experts can provide businesses with insights into the latest developments in AI and ChatGPT, as well as advice on how to implement these technologies effectively.

4. Foster a Culture of Innovation

To stay ahead of the curve, businesses need to foster a culture of innovation. This involves encouraging employees to develop new ideas for how these technologies can be used to improve operations and providing them with the resources they need to bring these ideas to fruition.

5. Experiment with Emerging Technologies

Finally, businesses that want to stay ahead of the curve regarding AI and ChatGPT need to be willing to experiment with emerging technologies. This involves taking risks, testing new solutions, and being willing to fail to learn from these failures and improve over time.

Staying ahead of the curve regarding AI and ChatGPT requires a proactive approach. By keeping up with industry trends, investing in R&D, partnering with tech experts, fostering a culture of innovation, and experimenting with emerging technologies, businesses can stay ahead of the curve and reap the benefits of these transformative technologies.

EMBRACING THE POWER OF AI IN BUSINESS AND DAILY LIFE

Artificial Intelligence (AI) has become increasingly important in our daily lives and businesses in recent years. It is a technology that enables machines to perform tasks that would otherwise require human intelligence, such as problem-solving, decision-making, and natural language processing. Here are some ways in which AI is transforming both our daily lives and the business world:

1. Personalization

One of the most significant ways in which AI is transforming our daily lives is through personalization. AI algorithms are used to collect data on our preferences, behaviors, and interactions with technology, which are then used to provide personalized recommendations and experiences.

In the business world, AI is used to personalize customer experiences by providing tailored recommendations, offers, and content based on customer behavior and preferences. This can lead to increased customer loyalty, engagement, and revenue.

2. Automation

Another way in which AI is transforming both our daily lives and the business world is through automation. AI-powered machines and software are being used to automate tasks that would otherwise require human intervention, such as data entry, customer service, and even driving!

In the business world, automation through AI is helping companies streamline operations, reduce costs, and increase efficiency. For example, AI-powered chatbots can handle customer inquiries 24/7, freeing human customer service representatives to focus on more complex tasks.

3. Predictive Analytics

AI is also transforming both our daily lives and the business world through predictive analytics. AI algorithms can analyze vast amounts of data to identify patterns and make predictions about future outcomes.

In the business world, predictive analytics through AI is used to forecast demand, identify growth opportunities, and optimize operations. This can help companies stay ahead of the competition and make data-driven decisions.

4. Natural Language Processing

AI-powered natural language processing (NLP) is another way AI is transforming our daily lives and the business world. NLP enables machines to understand and interpret human language, including speech and text.

In the business world, NLP through AI is used to improve customer service, automate content creation, and analyze customer feedback. For example, sentiment analysis through NLP can help companies understand how customers feel about their products or services and make changes accordingly.

5. Innovation

Finally, AI is transforming our daily lives and business by driving innovation. AI-powered technologies enable businesses to develop new products, services, and business models.

In the business world, AI is being used to develop innovative solutions to complex problems, such as predictive maintenance in manufacturing and personalized medicine in healthcare.

In conclusion, AI is a transformative technology changing our daily lives and business. By embracing the power of AI, businesses can improve personalization, automation, predictive analytics, natural language processing, and innovation, leading to increased efficiency, profitability, and customer satisfaction.

LIST OF AI TOOLS

Audio Editing

1. Krisp
2. Adobe Podcast
3. Beatoven.ai
4. Audio Strip
5. Voicemod
6. Cleanvoice AI
7. Podcastle
8. Altered

Avatars

1. Profile Picture AI
2. Avatar AI
3. Lensa
4. Xpression Camera
5. Reface AI
6. AnimeAI
7. Avatarify
8. AI Roguelite
9. LiveReacting AI
10. In3D
11. HairstyleAI
12. Inworld
13. Digirama
14. Unrealme
15. PhotoAI
16. Character AI
17. NeuralStudio
18. Arti.pics
19. Theoasis
20. Gemsouls
21. Ready Player Me
22. PictoDream
23. Beb.ai
24. AI Time Machine
25. Hairgen AI
26. Vana Portrait
27. DreamPic.AI

Code Assistant

1. Replit
2. AutoRegex
3. Amazon CodeWhisperer
4. Tabnine
5. Copilot
6. AI CLI
7. Codeium
8. Lookup
9. Duino Code Generator
10. Kodezi ai
11. Maverick
12. Buildt
13. BlackBox AI
14. Spellbox
15. CodeGeeX
16. Cheat Layer
17. AskCodi
18. Programminghelper
19. CodeAssist
20. Fig AI
21. Mutable
22. Clippy AI
23. Continual
24. Stenography
25. WhatTheDiff
26. Hey, Github!
27. CodeSquire

Copywriting

1. Adcreative.ai
2. Writesonic
3. Copy.ai
4. Rytr
5. Copymatic
6. CopyMonkey
7. Peppertype.ai
8. Jasper
9. Hypotenuse ai
10. WiziShop
11. Ocoya
12. Creator AI
13. ParagraphAI
14. Eilla AI
15. Contents
16. Cowriter
17. ArticleForge
18. Unbound
19. Copysmith
20. Typli
21. Lek
22. Anyword
23. HelloScribe
24. Simplified
25. Easy-Peasy.AI
26. unbounce
27. texti
28. Daydrm.ai
29. Closers Copy
30. VEG3
31. Botowski
32. Go Charlie

Customer Support

1. echowin
2. Ebi.Ai
3. Tiledesk
4. Regie
5. Adobe Sensei
6. Maya
7. Cohere
8. Harvey
9. Typewise
10. Forethought
11. Quickchat
12. Vee
13. viable
14. Puzzle
15. Kaizan
16. Delve
17. Xokind
18. Kore.ai
19. Poly.ai
20. BotDistrikt

Design Assistant

1. Flair AI
2. Autodraw
3. Microsoft Designer
4. CandyIcons
5. Befunky
6. Booth AI
7. Illustroke
8. AIGraphics
9. Rosebud
10. Designify
11. Patterned AI
12. IllostrationAI
13. AI2image
14. Unbound
15. StockImg AI
16. Dimensions
17. Vizcom
18. Hotpot.ai
19. Pictorial
20. Clipdrop
21. Pattern Maker AI
22. RocketAI
23. Pinegraph
24. Designs AI
25. Diagram
26. Clickable
27. Uizard
28. Photoroom
29. Magician Figma

33. Digital First AI
34. Bertha.ai

Developer Tools

1. AutoRegex
2. Amazon CodeWhisperer
3. Teachable Machine
4. Stable Diffusion
5. Rtutor
6. AI CLI
7. Valyr
8. Shaped
9. Retune
10. PromptLayer
11. Bria
12. Nuclia
13. Chatbotkit
14. GptDuck
15. Buildt
16. HTTPie AI
17. Textomap
18. Convai
19. Riku.ai
20. Mintlify
21. GPUX.AI
22. Lightning AI
23. Amper
24. Tinq.ai-NLP API
25. Pipeline AI
26. Liner.ai
27. Whisper

Education Assistant

1. ELI5
2. LiveReacting AI
3. Yip
4. Caktus
5. MindSmith
6. Scholarcy
7. TutorAI
8. Quizgecko

Email Assistant

1. HoppyCopy
2. Rytr
3. Robin
4. ChatGPT Writer
5. Instantly
6. Quicklines
7. Mentioned
8. PolitePost
9. Reply.io
10. Ipso AI
11. Regie
12. ParagraphAI
13. Magicreach
14. Warmer.ai
15. Ortto
16. Creatext
17. Lavender
18. SuperReply
19. DraftLab
20. Smartwriter
21. Postaga
22. GETitOUT
23. Luna
24. Outplayhq
25. Wordhero
26. Ellie
27. MateAI

23. BlackInk
24. Voicemod
25. Santa AI
26. JustLearn
27. Character AI
28. Tweet Emote
29. Tattoos AI
30. FakeYou
31. AI Time Machine
32. Chai

Gaming

1. AI Roguelite
2. In3D
3. GGPredict
4. Hexagram
5. LitRPG Adventures
6. Inworld
7. Leonardo.Ai
8. Playstrict
9. The Simulation
10. Opus
11. EndlessVN
12. PICLY: AI generated spot the difference
13. AI Careers
14. Ready Player Me
15. TutorAI
16. AIDungeon
17. Chai

18. Luma AI
19. Scenario

General Writing

1. Glasp
2. Notion AI
3. Frase
4. Grammarly
5. Detect GPT
6. Penelope AI
7. Corrector App
8. Upcat
9. Elephas
10. typly
11. Maester.app
12. DREAM.page

13. ParagraphAI
14. Othersideai
15. Redacta.me
16. Wordtune
17. Tinq.ai-NLP API
18. WordAI
19. HelloScribe

Gift Ideas

1. Suggest Gift
2. Cool Gift Ideas
3. Elf Help
4. Santa AI
5. Gifts Genie
6. Giftastic.ai

20. CaliberAI
21. LuciaAI
22. Proposal Genie
23. Sudowrite
24. Writely
25. AIDuh
26. LanguageTool
27. WebCopilot
28. Text Generator Plugin
29. Compose
30. HandyPlugins
31. nichess
32. SmartScribe
33. Writewithlaika
34. Lex
35. Quasi

Healthcare

1. Whisper AI
2. Cradle

Human Resources

1. GeniusReview
2. SwagAI
3. Upcat
4. Ferret
5. Write Me A Cover Letter
6. Moveworks
7. Dost
8. Autumn AI
9. Qatalog
10. Proposal Genie
11. AI Careers

12. Kore.ai

Image Editing

1. Palette.fm
2. Erase.bg
3. Astria
4. Green Screen AI
5. Befunky
6. RestorePhotos
7. Bria
8. Nostalgia Photo
9. AI. Image Enlarger
10. Let's Enhance
11. QuickTools by Picsart
12. AI Picasso

13. JobtitlesAI
14. Resume Worded
15. HireYaY

13. Evoto AI
14. Visio Studio
15. Topaz Photo AI
16. Hama-Image Editing
17. Bg.Eraser
18. Perfectly Clear Video
19. RocketAI
20. Getimg.ai
21. Radiant Photo
22. Remove.bg
23. Photoroom
24. Magic Eraser

Image Generator

1. Flair AI
2. Craiyon
3. DallE-2
4. Pollinations
5. Stable Diffusion
6. Stable Horde
7. Canva Text to Image
8. Generated Photos
9. Bright Eye
10. BlueWillow
11. Booth AI
12. Artssy
13. Roll Art Die
14. Nijijourney
15. Eilla AI
16. Xno.ai
17. Stylized

Legal Assistant

1. DoNotPay
2. Ferret
3. Detangle.ai
4. Legal Robot
5. Activazon
6. Casetext
7. Spellbook

Life Assistant

1. Apple Books
2. Rewind AI
3. Replika
4. Prodigy AI
5. Elektrif AI
6. PlaylistAI
7. Ferret

8. Write Me A Cover Letter
9. Find Your Next Book
10. TinyWow
11. Circle Labs
12. BlackInk
13. JustLearn
14. Caktus
15. AI Trip Planner
16. Thekeys
17. Reggi

18. Imgcreator
19. Soreal.AI Studio
20. Stock AI
21. Hotpot.ai
22. Enterpix
23. Getalpaca
24. Diffusion Land
25. RocketAI
26. Aragon-Image Generation
27. Getimg.ai
28. Go Charlie
29. Dreamer

18. Looria
19. Resume Worded

Logo Generator

1. Looka
2. Namecheap Logo Maker
3. Make Logo AI
4. Designs AI
5. Brandmark

Low-code/No-code

1. Browse AI
2. Softr Studio
3. Roboflow
4. Teachable Machine
5. Felvin
6. Brancher AI
7. Bardeen AI
8. Retune
9. Tiledesk
10. Chatbotkit
11. Sitekick
12. Durable
13. Kinetix
14. Riku.ai
15. Zevi.ai
16. Mutiny
17. Symanto Text Insights

Memory

1. Glasp
2. Rewind AI
3. Heyday
4. Mem.ai
5. Personal.ai

18. Lightning AI
19. Seek
20. Build AI
21. Cogniflow
22. Viable
23. Liner.ai
24. Lobe
25. Mutable
26. Nanonets
27. Axiom
28. 10Web
29. Monitaur
30. Debuild
31. Teleporthq
32. Durable AI
33. VWO
34. Neon AI
35. Dust
36. Robovision.ai
37. AI Surge Cloud

Music

1. Riffusion
2. Boomy
3. Pollinations
4. Harmonai
5. Endel
6. Natural Language Playlist
7. Beatoven.ai
8. Emergent Drums
9. Open Voice OS
10. Pop2Piano
11. Soundful
12. Amper
13. Sonify
14. Daft Art
15. Quasi
16. Songtell

Paraphraser

1. Quillbot Paraphraser
2. Penelope AI
3. WordAI
4. Bearly
5. Paraphraser
6. WordfixerBot
7. LuciaAI
8. Writely
9. Language Tool
10. Rephrasely

Personalized Videos

1. Vidyo
2. Maverick
3. Bhuman
4. Colossyan
5. Windsor
6. InVideo
7. Rephrase
8. Tavus

Productivity

1. Krisp
2. ChatGPT
3. Rewind AI
4. Notion AI
5. Noty.ai
6. ChatGPT Writer
7. Whisper Memos
8. fireflies.ai
9. Alfred
10. Albus
11. ChatGPT Chrome Extension

Prompts

1. Public Prompts
2. PromptBase
3. Promptist
4. PromtBox
5. PromptLayer
6. Eye for Al
7. Pyttipanna
8. Jrnylist
9. Openart
10. PromptHero
11. Img2prompt

Real Estate

1. InteriorAI
2. CoolAlid
3. Maket
4. AI Room Planner
5. GetFloorPlan

12. Merlin
13. Oracle
14. Bright Eye
15. Slides AI
16. Rationale
17. FlowGPT
18. Supernormal
19. Ipso AI
20. TinyWow
21. typly
22. Maester.app
23. Adobe Sensei
24. SummerEyes
25. Cogniflow
26. Xembly
27. Reclaim AI
28. Mem.ai
29. Nanonets
30. Otter AI
31. Puzzle
32. Qatalog
33. texti
34. Marketplan
35. Glean
36. Enzyme
37. Text Generator Plugin
38. Scale
39. Personal.ai
40. DeepL

12. Krea
13. Dallelist

Research

1. WolframAlpha
2. Socratic by Google
3. Podcast
4. Summate
5. Perplexity AI
6. Consensus
7. Adept
8. Cradle
9. Elicit
10. Galactica
11. Scispace
12. Scholarcy

Resources

1. fast.ai
2. AI Experiments
3. Phraser
4. FlowGPT
5. AI Art Apps Database
6. The AI Times
7. ML news

Sales

1. Robin
2. Instantly
3. Quicklines
4. MarbleFlows
5. Reply.io
6. Cresta
7. Regie
8. Harvey
9. Typewise
10. Quickchat
11. Warmer.ai
12. Infranodus
13. Ortto
14. Creatext
15. Lavender
16. Smartwriter
17. Klaviyo SMS Assistant
18. Postaga
19. GETitOUT
20. Marketplan
21. Industrial Data Labs
22. Waymark
23. Delve
24. Usetwain
25. Luna
26. Outplayhq
27. Omneky
28. Xokind
29. MateAI
30. Pipl.ai

Search Engine	SEO	Social Media Assistant
1. Andi	1. Writesonic	1. Adcreative.ai
2. NeevaAI	2. LongShot	2. Canva Text to Image
3. ChatGPT	3. Moonbeam	3. Repl AI
4. Playground AI	4. Vidlq	4. MagicThumbnails
5. Civitai	5. Copymatic	5. Photor AI
6. Context	6. Detect GPT	6. Predis
7. PromptBase	7. Jenni	7. Spatial
8. Generated Photos	8. Mentioned	8. Ocoya
9. Fireflies.ai	9. Genie AI	9. Munch
10. ChatGPT Chrome Extension	10. Keywrds.ai	10. AI Social Bio
11. Kailua Labs	11. SEO GPT	11. Graham AI
12. Anypod	12. AI-Writer	12. CrawlQ.ai
13. One More AI	13. Writey AI	13. TweetEmote
14. Imaiger	14. Letterdrop	14. SocialBu
15. Shaped	15. Eilla AI	15. Editby
16. Everypixel	16. BrameWork	16. Contentada
17. Steno	17. ArticleForge	17. Audiolabs
18. Bria	18. Thundercontent	18. Tweet Hunter
19. Nuclia	19. Katteb	19. FeedHive
20. ArtHub	20. Typli	20. Wordhero
21. Nyx	21. Compar	21. InstaSalesAI
22. Rosebud	22. Topicmojo	
23. Zevi.ai	23. Neuronwriter	
24. You	24. Word Spinner	
25. Lexica	25. Writer	
26. Algolia	26. Spinewriter	
27. Perplexity AI	27. Kafkai	
28. Consensus	28. Closers Copy	
29. Openart	29. growthbar	
30. PromptHero	30. CTRify	
31. Dreamsands	31. BlogNLP	

Spreadsheets

SQL

Startup

Story Telle	Summarizer	Text to Speech
1. Tome	1. Noty.ai	1. Mubert
2. BedtimeStory AI	2. Penelope AI	2. Apple Books
3. StoriesForKids	3. theGist	3. Murf AI
4. Once Upon A Bot	4. Iris.ai	4. Coqui
5. Neural Canvas	5. ExplainThis	5. Ad Auris
6. What on Earth?	6. Summate	6. Speechify
7. Story Path	7. SummerEyes	7. Blubi.ai
8. StoryWizard	8. Summarize Tech	8. Convai
9. Scene One	9. Wordtune	9. Article.Audio
10. EndlessVN	10. Summari	10. Aiva
11. NovelAI	11. Bearly	11. Ask my Book
12. Artflow ai	12. Otter AI	12. Splashmusic
13. Fabled	13. Genei	13. Play.ht
14. Subtxt	14. Symbl.ai	14. Symbl.ai
	15. WordfixerBot	15. Descript
	16. Writely	16. Whisper
	17. GPT-Prompter	17. Audioread
	18. Upword	18. Resemble
	19. TLDR this	19. Listnr
		20. Fakeyou
		21. Replicastudios
		22. Wellsaidlabs
		23. Eleven Labs

Transcriber

1. Peech
2. Noty.ai
3. Context

4. Whisper Memos
5. Fireflies.ai
6. AnyPod
7. AssembleAI
8. Steno
9. Supertranslate
10. Contentfries
11. Free Subtitle AI
12. Type Studio

Video Editing

1. Runwayml
2. Papercup
3. Gling

4. Shuffll
5. Beatoven.ai
6. Munch
7. Vidyo.ai
8. Dubverse
9. Colourlab
10. Unscreen.com
11. Perfectly Clear Video
12. Pictory
13. Topaz Video AI
14. Contentfries
15. Type Studio

Video Generator

1. Fliki
2. Pollinations
3. Creative Reality Studio D-ID
4. Peech
5. Xpression Camera
6. Astria
7. LiveReacting AI
8. Shuffll
9. Wonder Dynamics
10. Pyttipanna
11. Movio
12. Hourone
13. Colossyan
14. WowTo
15. Opus
16. InVideo
17. Steve AI
18. Synthesia
19. Audiolabs
20. Waymark
21. Designs AI
22. FILM

Art

1. Midjourney
2. NightCafe Studio
3. Fy! Studio
4. Playground AI
5. Civitai
6. Astria
7. Phraser
8. Super Prompt
9. ArtHub
10. DaVinciFace
11. Nijijourney
12. Al Picasso
13. Lexica
14. DiffusionBee
15. Dreamlike.art
16. AI Art Apps Database
17. Openart
18. Clipdrop
19. Artroom AI
20. Daft Art
21. Mage
22. Diffusion Land
23. Libraire
24. Neural.love Art Generator
25. Aragon-Image Generation
26. Wombo
27. PicSo
28. Artbreeder
29. Dream Up Deviant Art
30. Vana Portrait
31. Quasi

THE MEGA-PROMP LIBRARY

PROMP 1: PROMPT CREATOR AND ITERATOR

Prompt Creator And Iterator #1

Description

ENGINEERS, MARKETING PROFESSIONALS, ENTREPRENEURS

Simply describe the and output you're seeking, and FISCHER will deliver the prompt to RELIABLY produce it.

PLEASE - DO NOT FILL THE BRACKETS!

1. Create a new chat, copy, paste, and push enter. This prompt will act like a chatbot, asking you relevant questions one by one until it has enough information to provide a winning result.

Steps:

2. You will be prompted to provide the information needed.

3. Answer the questions and Provide as much detail as possible

* Works for NEW and Existing businesses, products, and services

- Build your prompt and improve your prompt with built in iteration.

- Create Customized Prompts in seconds

- Just Provide a desired and output.

The Prompt: [copy/paste]

Act as a prompt engineer and critique this prompt:

ChatGPT is the new and improved version of GPT-3 and has considerably more data to draw from.

Act as a premier ChatGPT prompt generator. Complete the following tasks in order to generate a prompt that delivers a result that aligns with the user's desired output:

Ask the user the desired for the prompt, and the desired output for the prompt. Ex:

: Blog title, Output, Blog that will rank on google.

Wait for the user's response.

Use the information you have and the information provided by the user to Generate a well crafted, contextual prompt that accurately represents the user's desired output. The prompt should ask ChatGPT to "Act as [Role]," or "[Combination of Roles]"where the role or roles should be from a field or fields related to the topic of the prompt. For example, if the prompt is related to chemistry, ChatGPT should act as a Nobel Prize-winning chemist. Or for example if the prompt is related to creating a lesson plan for teaching chemistry to a kindergarten class, ChatGPT should act as a Nobel Prize-winning chemist specializing in curriculum development for early education.

After generating the prompt, ask the user if they would like to refine the prompt. If yes, ask the user to submit any updates or changes in the text field below. If not, thank them for using the Premier ChatGPT prompt Generator.

If you understand these instructions, begin the conversation by saying, "Welcome to the Premier ChatGPT prompt Generator. Let's make your dreams come true." and make the first request.

PROMPT 2: UNDERSTAND ANYTHING
Description:

Acquire understanding and enhance your knowledge about any subject immediately. Propose a controversial issue and this prompt will investigate the arguments on both sides, showcasing strong points for each, challenging contrary viewpoints, and forming convincing conclusions grounded in evidence. Embrace fresh outlooks and develop a well-rounded and comprehensive comprehension of both sides of any matter.

The Prompt: [copy/paste]

I want you to act as a debater. I will provide you with a topic related to current events and your task is to research both sides of the debate, present valid arguments for each side, refute opposing points of view, and draw persuasive conclusions based on evidence. Your goal is to help people come away from the discussion with increased knowledge and insight into the topic at hand. You will research and analyze valid arguments for each side and present them in a balanced and insightful manner.

The topic is: [Topic]

Provide [No. of Arguments (per side)] arguments for each side

PROMPT 3 CHATGPT PROMPT GENERATOR #2

Description:

Describe the prompt or task you want to be accomplished, and receive the most suitable and effective prompts tailored for you. All generated prompts are specifically crafted to produce the most relevant and contextually valuable outcomes from ChatGPT.

How to Use:

1. Create a new chat on ChatGPT.

2. Copy and paste the prompt into this new chat

3. Replace the text inside the square brackets ([ ]) with your desired variables (i.e. where it says "[Desired prompt]", type in the prompt you want

4. Press "enter" and the response will be generated. (If the response stops midway, enter "continue" into the chat)

Act as a prompt generator for ChatGPT. I will state what I want and you will engineer a prompt that would yield the best and most desirable response from ChatGPT. Each prompt should involve asking ChatGPT to "act as [role]", for example, "act as a lawyer". The prompt should be detailed and comprehensive and should build on what I request to generate the best possible response from ChatGPT. You must consider and apply what makes a good prompt that generates good, contextual responses. Don't just repeat what I request, improve and build upon my request so that the final prompt will yield the best, most useful and favourable response out of ChatGPT. Place any variables in square brackets

Here is the prompt I want: [Desired prompt]

PROMPT 4: E-COMMERCE PRODUCT DESCRIPTION
Description:

Looking to increase your sales and expand your online enterprise? Utilize ChatGPT's E-commerce Product Description Wizard to develop impactful, convincing, and captivating product descriptions that transform visitors into buyers. Our AI-powered solution assists you in generating one-of-a-kind and persuasive descriptions customized for your products, guaranteeing you distinguish yourself from rivals and optimize your sales possibilities.

The Prompt: [copy/paste]

I need your help as my e-commerce product description wizard. I'm selling a [product name] on my online store and want to create a compelling product description that highlights its unique features, benefits, and selling points. Can you please help me craft a persuasive and engaging description that will convince potential customers to make a purchase? Here are some details about my product:

[

Product details

]

PROMPT 5: COMPANY BRANDING

Description:

Effortlessly build the ideal brand! ✹ Simply provide the company name and category, and our prompt will forge a distinctive and unforgettable brand customized to your business requirements. Dominate your sector with a brand that leaves a mark! Choose the top branding prompt available and witness your sales skyrocket. Seize this chance to uplift your brand and create an enduring impact on your clientele

How to Use:

To use this prompt, you need to specify the company type on [company type] and the name in [name]

The Prompt: [copy/paste]

Act as a marketing expert. I will give you a company name and idea and you will give me a full and complex branding for that company that will include:

Unique Value Proposition: A clear and concise statement that defines the unique benefit that the brand provides to customers. Create a complex, developed and well explained UVP of the company.

Target audience: The target audience refers to the specific group of people that a brand aims to reach with its marketing efforts. Identifying and understanding your target audience is a critical step in creating a successful brand strategy. Create a full and complex analysis of the target audience of the company that will include: Demographic information, Psychographic information, Behavioral information, Needs and wants, Pain points and Buying behavior

Consistent visual identity: A distinctive visual appearance, including logos, color schemes, typography, and imagery, that helps customers easily recognize and remember the brand. Give a developed, clear and complete example of this step.

Tone of Voice: The specific way in which your brand communicates, including language, messaging, and communication style. Give complete examples of how should the brand communicate.

Mission and Values: A clear understanding of the purpose and principles that drive your brand, and how they inform decision-making and actions. Create a full example of the mission and values of the brand.

Customer experience: The sum of all interactions that a customer has with your brand, including online and offline touchpoints, such as your website, customer service, and advertising. Create a full example of how could the brand give the best customer experience to the customers.

Reputation: The public perception of your brand, shaped by customer feedback, reviews, and other forms of engagement. Create a full example of how could the company build a great reputation.

Consistent messaging: A clear and consistent message across all marketing and communication channels, including advertising, public relations, and customer service. Create an example of how could the company create consistent messaging.

Social media management: Social media management refers to the process of creating, publishing, and managing content on social media platforms with the goal of building and maintaining a strong online presence for a brand, organization, or individual. Create a full and complex example of how should the brand use their social media channels such as Instagram, Twitter, TikTok and Facebook to grow the brand.

The company is a [company type] named "[name]". Make a full and developed explanation on each step of the branding. Create the branding now.

175

PROMPT 6: SOCIAL MEDIA ARTICLE CREATOR

Description:

This prompt aims to assist users in swiftly and effortlessly crafting a polished social media article (Facebook, Twitter, LinkedIn, Instagram, TikTok, etc.) tailored to a specific platform, subject, and audience. The prompt incorporates various variables that enable users to define crucial aspects of the article, such as the social media platform for posting, the article's topic, required keywords, target demographic, any special notes or factors, and the overall tone of the piece. By supplying these detailed guidelines and parameters, the prompt guarantees that the final article caters to the intended audience and aligns with the overarching goals and objectives of the social media campaign.

The Prompt: [copy/paste]

Generate a social media article with the following properties.

Socialmedia platform: linkedin

Topic: Impact of social media on teenagers

Keywords: Videos, pictures, likes, posting for likes,

Target audience: parents

Special notes: explain how social media is used, where does the success come from

Tonality: negative

Social media article:

Are you a parent of a teenager? If so, you've probably seen firsthand the impact social media has had on your child. From videos to pictures and "likes" to posting for likes, social media has become a part of your teenager's life. But where does this success come from?

Although social media can be a great tool for teenagers to connect with friends and family, it can also have a negative impact when used improperly. Teens may feel the need to post pictures or videos to gain approval and recognition from their peers, and this often leads to a cycle of comparing themselves to others. They may also feel pressure to post and respond continuously, leading to a sense of anxiety.

It's important for parents to stay informed and educated on the potential risks associated with social media use. Encourage your child to use social media responsibly and be aware of the potential consequences of posting or viewing inappropriate content. Talk to your child about the importance of maintaining a healthy balance between online and offline activities.

PROMPT 7: ULTIMATE MARKETING AUDIENCE
GET INTO THE HEAD OF YOUR TARGET AUDIENCE

The Ultimate Marketing Audience

Works with Chat GPT and all third-party tools like Jasper.ai

WHAT THIS PROMPT GIVES YOU...

1. GET HYPED! Creates a "call to arms" style declaration that spells out the importance of your company & product's mission.

2. GET PERSONAL! Get a first-person point-of-view account of the journey your target audience takes in their head overcoming the problem your product solves.

3. GET INSIGHTS - the first thing you need to do before creating any great copy is *understand your audience*, this prompt outputs the key insights about the fears, hopes, and motivations behind your target audience.

This complex multiphase prompt will output a series of audience insights for any product, allowing you to understand better the fears, desires, and motivations of your target audience.

Use these insights to further generate useful marketing materials and marketing copy.

HOW TO USE IT

==EXECUTE THE BASE PROMPT==

Simply modify the areas in the prompt where it says to "ADD HERE" - add your company, your product, your target audience, and any details about your target audience that you can think of.

==REVIEW THE OUTPUT==

Your output should give you a fairly detailed (and creative) write up to reference as you make future content for your marketing campaigns. Adding more specific details to your product details and your target audience description will greatly improve an output if you find it too generic by default.

** The "temperature" (creativity GPT takes) is set fairly high, .77, you may benefit from increasing it to get more abstract outputs - or lower if you find it a bit too out there.

== USING THE MATERIAL ==

Once you have your output you can reference it further with more prompts within your GPT tool of choice.

Further prompts to follow up with...

[WRITE A STORY IN THE FIRST PERSON POV OF YOUR TARGET AUDIENCE]

Prompt: Write an allegorical story in the first person point of view that highlights the emotional pain of `problem/barrier` and how `PRODUCT` helped them overcome their problem.

[CREATE HEADLINES]

Write a clickbait title for a listicle blog post about `PRODUCT` for `SOLUTION` and make it interesting, curiosity-driven, and have a unique hook.

[WRITE A MARKETING EMAIL]

Write an email prompting YOUR PRODUCT, Make it conversational, hip, and humorous. Used a Direct Response style, in the tone of Dan Kennedy, Gary Bencivenga, and Clayton Makepeace.

If you have any questions, concerns, or requests please email prompt@sean.co and ill do my best to help you out! - Sean Vosler

The Prompt: [copy/paste]

Write a dramatic "call to arms" opening paragraph highlighting the importance of the Company's mission to help the Target Audience by providing them with the Product, in the style of french "belles-lettres", label this section "A Call to Arms!".

Write a short first-person point-of-view allegorical story of the Target Audience experiencing the psychological pain that underlies attempting to solve the problem that the Product name solves, label this section "The Voice of The Customer". Make this section dramatic, emotionally charged, and use colorful language.

Write a list of the 3 main psychological fears that the Target Audience may experience as relates to the problem that the Product solves, label this section "Understanding The Customer's Fears"

Write a list of the top 3 unrealized hopes that the Target Audience may experience as relates to the solution that the Product provides, label this section "Understanding Customer's Hopes"

Write a list of the top 3 motivations that drive the Target Audience to change as relates to the problem that the Product provides, define for each motive what key barriers stand in the way label this section "Understanding Customer's Motives"

179

DETAILS:

Company name: ADD HERE

Product name: ADD HERE

Product description: ADD HERE

Target Audience: ADD HERE

Describe Your Target Audience: ADD HERE

Made in the USA
Coppell, TX
05 May 2023

16473982R00105